Portrait of a General

George Armstrong Custer
and the Battle of the Little Big Horn

by
W. DONALD HORN

Printing by: Southeast Publications USA, Inc.
1-800-832-3292
Copyright © 1998, Don Horn Publications, West Orange, NJ
All Rights Reserved.

ISBN 0-9639912-2-1

For Ann

Introduction

What you are about to read is not a biography of George Armstrong Custer, but rather a positive study of him. Custer's critics today have become so obsessed with his defeat at the Battle of The Little Big Horn, that a complete and accurate picture of Custer has become difficult to find. Acknowledging the fact that there can be two sides to every story, person or situation, this study will deal only with the positive side of George Armstrong Custer.

Acknowledgment

In 1980 I published a book entitled *Witnesses For The Defense Of General George Armstrong Custer*. The work contained a brief history of the General and the testimony of ninety-eight witnesses, who knew him personally. In this new work, I have used much of the research that went into that project.

In creating *Portrait of a General*, I remain indebted to several people, who responded to my call for help when I was doing my original research for *Witnesses For The Defense*. Invaluable were two late dear friends Dr. Lawrence A. Frost of Monore, Michigan and John M. Carroll of Bryan, Texas; Al Clark, who, when I met him, was cataloging the Elizabeth Custer Collection at Eastern Montana College; the late Kenneth Rapp, who gave so generously of his time, while serving as assistant Archivist at West Point. I also note with appreciation all the National Park Service employees, who were serving at Custer Battlefield National Monument during the time I was doing my research, for allowing me access to the archives at the Battlefield museum.

To my friend Brice Custer, a direct descendent of General Custer's Brother Nevin Custer, I extend sincerest gratitude for consenting to do the introduction to this book. And a thank you to Barney King, whose fine drawing of Custer on the Yellowstone decorates the cover of this book.

I also owe many thanks to Tom Bookwalter, Bill Boyes and Louise Barnett who read my manuscript and gave me a great deal of help and advice. I thank my son-in-law David McMillin for the design phase of this work. Thank you Meredith Lisagor for editing *Portrait of a General*. You were necessary. And finally, thank you friend Tom O'Neil for your constant encouragement and support.

W. DONALD HORN
WEST ORANGE, N.J.

Forward

There have been countless numbers of books written about "Custer's Last Stand," as well as a considerable number of movies concerning this dramatic event in American history. Though much of the written material has been of a critical nature, I believe it has been the motion picture that has had the most impact on the public's view of my great-great uncle General George Armstrong Custer. I know that I am correct when I state that few of Hollywood's efforts have adhered to historical accuracy when dealing with George Custer and I feel strongly that films, particularly those made in the last few decades, are responsible for the deteriorating image of a man who had previously been held in such high esteem by his countrymen.

Anyone who wishes an informed opinion of George Custer needs historically accurate information...information that is not restricted to the final days or hours of his life. Fortunately, there have been—and continue to be—individuals who have studied the career of my famed ancestor and have done so with a diligent devotion to historical accuracy as well as scholarly objectivity. No one better fits this description than the author of this book, W. Donald Horn.

His book provides a quick, factual review of the more important phases of the "Custer story," including his phenomenal performance in the Civil War. Perhaps more importantly, the author has punctuated each chapter with quotations from the writings of Custer contemporaries which amply refute the grotesque image presented by Hollywood.

Speaking for the Custer family, I would like to take this opportunity to publicly express our appreciation for those who continue the search for the truth and to W. Donald Horn in particular for his many years of informed defense of the competence and character of George Armstrong Custer.

BRICE C. CUSTER
GEORGETOWN, TEXAS
28 MAY 1997

Preface

Georacter George Armstrong Custer was an Ohio farm boy, who wanted to be a soldier. He would become one of America's most remembered. Custer accomplished much in his thirty-six years and six months of life. At the time of his death at the Little Big Horn, he was one of America's most celebrated military heroes, having acquired an enviable reputation as a youthful leader of Union Cavalry in America's Civil War. Consider how his Civil War adversaries, as well as his comrades, remembered him.

JOSEPH B. KERSHAW
National Archives

CONFEDERATE GENERAL JOSEPH B. KERSHAW

I look upon General Custer as one of the best cavalry officers that this or any other country ever produced.[1]

JAMES B. GORDON
National Archives

CONFEDERATE GENERAL JAMES B. GORDON

...every American citizen should be proud of General George Armstrong Custer.[2]

REVEREND THEODORE J. YOUNG
CHAPLAIN 1ST CONNECTICUT CAVALRY

> I cannot express my gratefulness to the Almighty that he should have made you such a General and such a man. I rejoice with the Third Division, with the army, with the whole country in the splendid military genius that has made your name glorious in the history of war.[3]

CAPTAIN E.D. WOODBURY
1ST VERMONT CAVALRY

> At the close of the war I was Acting Adjutant of my regiment, the 1st Vermont Cavalry and many times saw General Custer. In common with all our men I regard him as by far the best cavalry commander of the whole war, either Union or Confederate.[4]

PRIVATE W. H. BEEBE,
3RD NEW JERSEY CAVALRY, 2ND BRIGADE

> ...how his command adored him; how willing we were to follow where he led; the confidence we had in his judgement, and the assurance that when he struck a blow on the enemy, it would be a victory[5]

COLONEL JAMES H. KIDD
6TH MICHIGAN CAVALRY

> ...what Seydlitz was to Frederick the Great; what Prince Rupert was to Charles Stuart; what Joachim Murat was to Napoleon Bonaparte, what J.E.B. Stuart was to Robert E. Lee; what Sheridan was to Ulysses S. Grant; such was Custer to Philip H. Sheridan.[6]

Subordinate officers in Custer's Michigan Cavalry Brigade probably gave their youthful leader his greatest testimonial. When Custer received his promotion to Major General and was given command of the Third Cavalry Division, eighty-four officers of his old Michigan brigade officially requested transfer to the new command. They knew better than anyone else that their best chance for success and survival lay in remaining under the command of their youthful leader, George Armstrong Custer.[7]

If the information just related is accurate (and if one researches primary-source materials, they will find that it is quite accurate) why then, is George Armstrong Custer so maligned today? Why is he now so often portrayed as one of America's great villains? Could the reason be that in the latter part of his career, he fought Indians and not Rebels? Did Custer really change from his Civil War days, when he led cavalry so brilliantly, to the rash and reckless officer he is so often portrayed as today? Henry Capehart who served with Custer's 3rd Division from Winchester to Appomatox said, in a letter written in 1890 to Colonel Charles King, that Custer was counted on by some as rash because he dared while they dared not.

George Armstrong Custer was human...mere flesh and blood. He had the same human failings that you and I have. One might ask, was he not vain and egotistical? Perhaps he was. But is it a crime to be so? Was he a seeker of glory? Perhaps he was that also. What great soldiers are not? If vanity and egotism are to be considered undesirable traits, then let us be fair and consider Custer's fine qualities as well.

George Armstrong Custer was brave. No one, not even his detractors, will deny him that. George Custer was a leader of men. That's on the record for all to see. He was individual and spectacular. He was recognized and honored at such an early age that he can be considered super-human to have been able just to cope.

Of his capacity to love and care deeply, we know this, he was a doting husband, who wanted his wife near him at all times...in her eyes, he could do no wrong. He loved his family and wanted them physically close to him whenever possible. That fact would compound the Custer Family grief after the Battle at the Little Big Horn, for dead with the General on Last Stand Hill were his brothers Thomas and Boston, his nephew Harry Armstrong Reed and his brother-in-law James Calhoun.

Custer was an abidingly devoted son. He dearly loved and respected his Mother and Father. In a letter he wrote to his father from West Point, he freely offered, "I look back on the days spent under the family-roof as a period of pure happiness, and I feel thankful for such noble parents."[8] His devotion was met by his mother, who responded to another letter with, "When you speak of your boyhood home in your dear letter I had to weep for joy that the recollection was sweet in your memory."[9]

Custer took pride in himself and his regiment. Colonel Charles King, a contemporary of Custer, once wrote, "The way they move, you know in an instant that it is the 7th Cavalry."[10] Pride and performance reflect leadership.

From Bull Run to Appomattox, his career was like a shooting star, blazing its way across the heavens, appearing suddenly and then fading away in a spectacular flash. General of brigade at the age of twenty-three and a major general, commanding a division of cavalry in the Army of The Potomac, at twenty-five. George Custer rose to dazzling heights and had done so by an age at which most men's lives have scarcely begun.

On Sunday afternoon, June 25, 1876, at the age of thirty-six years and six months, his brilliant career came to a sudden and violent end on the heights overlooking the Little Big Horn River in what is now southeastern Montana. It was there that he and five companies of his fabled United States 7th Cavalry rode into immortality in a mystery-shrouded battle with Indians of the North American plains. No sooner had the smoke of battle drifted away than the controversy began. Who was at fault for this unbelievable disaster? America's most famous and glorious regiment of cavalry and its leader, the "Boy General" of the Civil War, George Armstrong Custer, "gone" by the hand of "hostile Indians" on the western plains.

After Custer's death at the Little Big Horn, he was considered a hero to most Americans. He was glorified in poetry and novels. He was the subject of countless paintings, and with the coming of the motion picture became one of its most popular subjects, though rarely depicted accurately. Somewhere along the line, however, the brilliant reputation so well earned by him during his military career began to tarnish. Americans, guilt-driven over questionable Indian policies of past governments, began to associate the name Custer with those policies. Because of this, George Armstrong Custer has today been accused of: roaming the West indiscriminately killing every Indian man, woman and child he could find; inept leadership; rashness; disobedience and cruelty. He has even been psychoanalyzed, in absentia, by the famous Dr. Charles Menninger.

This is all too convenient, too pat. A nation cannot and should not attempt to expiate its sins through a carefully selected hero of the past. Custer's loyal service to his country, which began with his four years of study at the United States Military Academy at West Point and continued into the Civil War, where he amassed an outstanding record, has been almost completely ignored. His years of service on the Western Frontier, which eventually led to the sacrifice of his life in the service of his country, today is met almost universally with satirical criticism. Neither George Armstrong Custer nor the American army were responsible for America's Indian Wars. Like all soldiers, they were men under orders from a higher authority and were obliged to carry out orders given them to the best of their ability. Custer was a professional soldier doing his country's bidding, and for that devotion to duty he has been accused by many modern day writers of perpetrating the cruelest of crimes against his fellow man. How did all this distortion come about? Has Custer become a symbol to the present generation of all that was bad in the development of the American West? A well known writer once stated in a long-ago issue of Life Magazine that the only way to cure the Indian ills of the past was to destroy the "Custer Myth." Where in heaven's name is the logic in such a proposal? The writer, however, was indeed prophetic, for Custer's reputation today has been all but destroyed.

Many authors have had a field day during the last half of the twentieth century questioning Custer's motives and ability. Deploring past governments' subjugation of the American Indian, they have found the perfect target in Custer, since he happened to serve that government at that time, was a popular folk hero of the day, and was the leading participant in the most famous battle of America's Indian Wars. These champions of the then oppressed American Indian are no doubt sincere in their attempt to uncover wrongs of the past, however, in their efforts, many have placed the blame for those wrongs where it does not belong. They have found it convenient to blame those who choose to follow the guidon rather than those who sent the guidon forth.

In condemning Custer, many writers have leaned heavily, without realizing it, on the letters of one man, Captain Frederick W. Benteen, a troop commander in Custer's 7th Cavalry. Benteen had little use for any of the officers he served with in the 7th and had a particularly bitter hatred for George Custer.[11] Over the years, his poison pen supplied most of the venom for Custer detractors. Colonel Charles A. Varnum, who served with Custer at the Little Big Horn as Chief of Scouts stated in an interview with Walter Mason Camp:

MAJOR MARCUS A. RENO
West Point

Custer was a young officer and was hated by Benteen and other of the old Civil War Colonels for the discipline maintained. While Custer was a spectacular man in some respects, he nevertheless was wide awake, full of push and withal, a very efficient officer. These qualities caused jealousy and hatred on the part of some. He had great endurance and energy and in all his military service he was always the leader. Benteen and Reno [Major Marcus A.

Reno, second in command in Custer's 7th
Cavalry] always hated him. Custer knew this
but was always considerate of them and was
always ready to do them favors.[12]

But how are we to know what George Armstrong
Custer was really like? The late great Custer Historian
Dr. Lawrence A. Frost stated in his comprehensive work,
General Custer's Libbie, "A rational judgement of George
Armstrong Custer can never be attained through the eyes
of his detractors alone. To know him well enough to reach
a sound and just conclusion as to his character, one
must see him through the eyes of his wife and friends."
One might respond. "Why rely on his wife and friends?"
Well, why not? Are we not to listen to the people who knew
him best?" Are we to disregard their testimony as biased
because they knew and loved him? What greater treasure
can a man accumulate in life than friends and what greater
tribute to a man than to have those friends give testimony
on his behalf.

The charge has been made by some historians that
there were those who served with Custer who were critical
of him, but would not give testimony against him while
his wife Elizabeth was alive. I submit that those historians
were opportunistic in citing respect for the dear lady as
a gag on criticism from some of Custer's own men. And
they were safe in peddling that speculation, since Elizabeth
Bacon Custer died on March 1, 1933 (two days before her
ninty-first birthday), and was survived by none of those
suggested to have had something to say against her husband. Furthermore, what of value could such detractors
tell the American public about George Armstrong Custer

that his closest companion and confident, his wife Libbie, did not already know? Surely not how the Battle of The Little Big Horn was fought; that was rehashed many times over in her lifetime. And surely not what he was "really like"; who but Libbie Custer would know George Armstrong Custer so completely.

Among Dr. Frost's Custer literature there is a book entitled, *Custer's Cavalry and the Campaign of '73*. It was the last of Dr. Frost's many books. Larry Frost and I were close friends. I thank goodness for the privilege of having known him. He was not only a dear friend, but was a dedicated and honest Custer scholar. I am honored that Dr. Frost chose to dedicate his final work to me. The dedication reads: "To Don Horn, who believes that this is the time for the truth to be known." What follows is my attempt to translate this belief into action.

W. D. H.
1998

BREVET MAJOR GENERAL GEORGE ARMSTRONG CUSTER
WEST POINT CLASS OF JUNE 1861

Author's Collection

The Birth of the Legend

George Armstrong Custer was born in the sleepy hamlet of New Rumley, Ohio on December 5, 1839. He was the first surviving son of widow Maria Ward Kirkpatrick and widower Emmanual Custer. Emmanual had taken Maria as his wife after the death of their spouses. George Armstrong would be followed in birth by three brothers Nevin, Thomas Ward, Boston and a sister Margaret. The Custers were a close-knit family, and would remain so all the days of their lives. Young George, affectionately called "Autie" by his family, was the centerpiece—all in the family adored him. Father Emmanual Custer was a blacksmith and the local justice of the peace. He was also a very vocal Democrat. If there was a political discussion taking place in New Rumley, you could be fairly certain that Emmanual Custer would be in the center of it.

John Giles, a cousin of Emmanual Custer, provides an early picture of the very young George Custer. Giles remembered walking with his cousin Emmanuel by a barnyard when they heard a child screaming. Little "Autie" appeared busting through a line of currant bushes with a huge gander fastened on his back.[1] It seems that the little fellow had been attracted to some goslings, and when he went for them the gander had alighted on him and was whipping him with his wings.

Another Giles remembrance of Custer in his formative years concerns young George's response to the "cornstalk militia" formed by the New Rumley locals. His father, a member of the group, usually took the boy to weekly drill, where little Autie would march behind the militiamen, imitating their every move. Giles was convinced that this early exposure to soldiering is what fueled George Custer's passion for a military career.

Custer's cousin Mary E. Snyder said that young George was particularly mischievous, and that his mother often said, if there was anything doing out of the ordinary, she could always lay the blame on him. Not that he was a vicious boy, said cousin Mary, he was just full of life and was always ready to do anything that had a semblance of daring in it. She remembered that all the Custer boys were possessed of a chivalrous nature, and George Armstrong particularly so.[2]

William O. Wirt, a boyhood friend of Custer, reported the young Custer was just a big-hearted whole-soul fellow as far back as he could recall.[3] Wirt remembered a conversation that his sister Elizabeth and Custer's cousin Lizzie Cunningham had had after Custer received his appointment to the Military Academy. Lizzie said to Elizabeth, "Wouldn't it be strange if George were to become a General?" Wirt remarked that both girls agreed that if anybody could arrive at that favored position it would be him.[4]

When Custer reached the age of twelve, he was sent to live with his half sister Lydia Reed in Monroe, Michigan. Monroe was the third largest city in the state of Michigan with better alternatives for young Custer's schooling. Father and Mother Custer agreed that this move would be in the best interest of their son. Besides that, sister Lydia was lonesome for the company of a Custer and young Autie had always been her favorite.

While living with the Reeds in Monroe, Custer attended Alfred Stebbin's Young Men's Academy. A Stebbin's Academy story that persists in Custer lore is that about Custer's habit of secreting military books inside his regular textbooks so he could read of the exploits of heroic soldiers when his attention should have been directed to the lesson at hand. Schoolmaster Stebbins always wore bedroom slippers during class so he could quietly approach students from behind and expose their inattentive ways. According to his classmates, Custer was one of Master Stebbins' favorite targets.

Lydia Reed insisted that along with his formal education, young Autie Custer attend church and Sunday School. Reverend Seth Reed, Pastor of the St. Paul Methodist Church, recorded the following in the Pastor's report of 1853-55:

PASTOR SETH REED
Author's Collection

While his [George Custer] deportment in church or Sunday School would be nearly so respectful that it could not well be reproved, yet it was so sly and concealed that he would plan fun for a half a dozen other boys older and larger than he to execute, while he would look as sober as a Deacon. Sometimes in prayer meeting we could hear, but could not see, small bird shot snapped from the thumb nails and rebounding over the carpet floor, while not a smile would appear on the face of any of them. We knew who was the promoter of such schemes, for George was easily their leader.[5]

It was during Custer's early years in Monroe that he first came in contact with his future wife, Elizabeth Bacon. Libbie—as she was lovingly called all her life—always enjoyed telling of her first encounter with the teenaged George Custer. Little Libbie, fives years Custer's junior, was swinging on the front gate of the Bacon home, and as Custer passed by she blurted out, "Hello, you Custer boy." After such a brash outburst, she ran into the house, overcome by embarrassment. It would be some years later that she would formally meet her future husband. Judge Daniel Bacon Libbie's father, was one of Monroe's leading citizens. He at first would not accept Custer as a proper suitor for his daughter. It was not so much Custer's station in life that bothered him, he said, but rather the fact that Custer had chosen a life in the military which could possibly expose his daughter to unthinkable hardships. George and Libbie's courtship would include a period during which they would have to use an intermediary for their correspondence. Judge Bacon did finally sanction the relationship, but only after Custer had earned the epaulets of a brigadier general and became a shining new star in the Civil War's galaxy of military heroes.

After receiving his formal education in Monroe, Custer returned to New Rumley and secured a teaching position in Hopewell Township. However, teaching school was only temporary for George Custer. He yearned for a military career...it is uncertain why. It could have been his youthful experience with the New Rumley Militia that enfluenced him or perhaps it was simply the clouds of war that hovered over the Nation in the late 1850's. Be that as it may, Custer successfully petitioned Ohio congressman

Jonathan Bingham for an appointment to the Military Academy at West Point. Bingham was to comment years later on Custer's letter of request:

**REP.
JONATHON
BINGHAM**
National Archives

I had not been in Congress long when I received a letter, that captivated me. Packed among my papers I have it yet, but, written over forty years ago, I remember every word. Written in a boyish hand, but firmly, legibly, it told me that the writer—a Democrat boy, that I might be under no misapprehension —wanted to be a soldier, wanted to go to West Point, and asked what steps he should take regarding it. Struck by its originality, its honesty, I replied at once.[6]

Custer entered The Military Academy at West Point in the Fall of 1857 and completed four years of required study. Custer is usually described as a dull, mischievous and slovenly cadet. Much has been made of the fact that he graduated last in a class of thirty four and of the great number of demerits or "skins" he accumulated during his undergraduate days. There is strong reason to believe that Custer might have escaped the dubious honor of "class goat" had his entire Plebe Class been graduated. With the possibility of armed conflict between the States edging closer, most all the Southern Cadets had resigned from the Academy and returned home to fight for their native states. Cadet Joseph Pearson Farley, a classmate of Custer's, tells us that the class of '61 originally numbered one hundred, then eighty, then sixty, then fifty and finally thirty-four.[7] Had the class stayed together, Cadet Custer might have enjoyed a standing at a comfortable—if not distant—remove from the bottom of the class. As far as demerits or skins were concerned, cadets were allowed one hundred per semester. Anymore than that number could result in dismissal. The West Point Archive records clearly show that Custer ceased to accumulate demerits each semester after he had received close to the number requiring dismissal. It appears, then, that the matter of demerit-accumulation may have been a game to the mischievous young cadet from Ohio. Most of Custer's infractions listed in the "skins book" in the West Point Archives were for such minor transgressions as: failure to have his hair combed; bouncing of his piece (rifle) when coming to attention; throwing snow balls; speaking while in ranks; cooking in his quarters after taps; throwing stones; late at parade; waist plate out of order, and belts twisted at inspection [8]

According to classmate Peter Michie, Custer was constantly in trouble with the school authorities. He said

**CADET
PETER MICHIE**
West Point Archives

Custer never saw an adjutant in full uniform that he did not suspect that he was the object of his search for the purpose of being placed under arrest. To have five minutes more of freedom, Custer would cut and run to delay the well known formula, "You are hereby placed under arrest and confined to your quarters by direction of the Superintendent."[9] With admiration Michie added that Custer had more fun, gave his friends more anxiety, walked more extra tours of guard duty, and came nearer being dismissed more often than any other cadet he ever knew. He said Custer believed that there were two positions of distinction, since he could not be the head of the class he used considerable ingenuity in establishing himself at the foot of the class.[10]

There can be little doubt that Custer was held in high esteem by his fellow classmates. Cadet E. Van Arsdale Andress of Newark, New Jersey said he would never cease to cherish the memory of George Custer—adding that Custer's boyish pranks and harmless frolics kept him [Custer] in constant hot water. Andress went on to say that Custer was beyond a doubt the most popular boy in his class.[11]

Cadet Morris Shaff, a classmate of Custer said that Custer was good natured and devoted to his friends. He was, Shaff reported, a joyous fellow, absolutely free of malice, hatred or revenge, attached to the friends of his youth and ceaselessly delighted in talking of his home.[12] In his book, *The Spirit of Old West Point*, Shaff tells of an incident involving Cadet Custer that occurred just before graduation. Custer, while acting

CADET MORRIS SHAFF
West Point Archives

as officer of the day, failed to separate two cadets who were brawling. Charges were preferred against him. Custer pleaded guilty and received only a reprimand. His lenient sentence, said the court, was handed down in consideration of his general good conduct as testified to by his immediate commander Lieutenant Hazen. In Shaff's view, it was fortunate for the country that things worked out as they did and Custer was permitted to remain at the Academy.

CHAPTER ONE
Epilogue

JUDGE R.M. VOORHEES
Voorhees was a classmate of George Custer in the New Rumley, Ohio elementary school.

> Despite the hard work of the farm, he [Custer] was a leader in sports, by nature manly, exuberant, with a noble knightly countenance.

This quote may be found in Henry Howe's A Talk With John Giles of Scio, Historical Collections of Ohio, Vol. 1
Norwalk, Ohio, Laning Printing Co., 1896 P. 900.

DR. GEORGE LYLE
Lyle was a classmate of George Custer in the New Rumley, Ohio elementary school.

> He [Custer] was an apt scholar, leader among the boys, mischievous, and full of practical jokes; withal very plucky.

This quote also maybe found in Henry Howe's *A Talk With John Giles of Scio.* P. 89

**CADET
TULLY
MCCREA**

West Point Archives

TULLY MCCREA

McCrea was Custer's roommate in his second year at West Point.

I remember how much I admired and partly envied Custer's free and careless way...it was alright with him whether he knew his lesson or not; he did not let it trouble him.

This qoute may be found in Catherine S. Crary's *Dear Belle*, Wesleyan University Press, Middletown, Connecticut. P.239

**THOMAS WARD CUSTER, BROTHER OF GEORGE CUSTER
WINNER OF TWO MEDALS OF HONOR IN THE CIVIL WAR.
THIS IS THE ONLY KNOWN PHOTOGRAPH SHOWING WOUNDS ON
THE RIGHT SIDE OF HIS FACE RECEIVED IN THAT WAR.**

Author's collection

The Civil War Years

I would not ask for a leave when all are needed.
It is my duty to take whatever position they
assign me. It is useless to hope the coming
struggle will be bloodless or of short duration.
Much blood will be spilled and thousands of
lives, at the least, lost. If it is my lot to fall in
the service of my Country and my Country's
rights I will have no regrets.

CADET GEORGE ARMSTRONG CUSTER
In a letter to his sister Lydia Ann from West Point [1]

In 1861 there was a pressing
need for army officers to train the new recruits that were
filling the ranks of the Union Army. West Point, therefore,
graduated two classes in 1861...the regularly scheduled class
and Custer's undergraduate class of 1862. Graduating a
year earlier than scheduled, Custer would get the advantage
of early participation in the war of Southern rebellion.
Custer's West Point record did leave much to be desired.
He personally described his undergraduate days as a
model to be avoided by future cadets. His West Point
record, however, would not be an indicator or predictor
of how he would perform in the stormy days immediately
ahead. After graduation, he was assigned to the cavalry
corps. Most Cadets with unimpressive academic records
were.

His first combat assignment was to the Second United States Cavalry. He led a platoon of that unit in the first Battle of Bull Run. Union forces were routed in that fight, but as reported by Custer's young orderly/trumpeter Joseph Fought:

> Custer never let up, never slackened control. Then when Arlington was reached and his company assigned to its camp, he snatched a few hours sleep beneath a tree...even while his name was being cited for bravery in the Capital.[2]

JOSEPH FOUGHT
Little Big Horn Battlefield Archives

According to Fought, Custer was a conspicuous figure from the first, attracting attention wherever he went.[3]

Custer's first assignment of importance was an appointment to the staff of General George McClellan, who at the time was commanding the Army of the Potomac. McClellan spoke of this appointment in a dispatch to President Abraham Lincoln:

> Soon after reaching the Chicahominy I took as one of my aides Lieutenant G. A. Custer as a reward for an act of daring gallantry.[4]

What was this act of "daring gallantry?" Custer along with several other Union officers were in their saddles on the banks of the Chicahominy River wondering how deep the water was. Suddenly, Custer jumped from his horse, waded to the middle of the stream, turned to his fellow officers, raised his arms and said, "this deep." When the incident was reported to General McClellan he immediately asked for Custer and offered him an appointment to his staff. McClellan later said that Custer seemed to place little importance on what he had done, but eagerly accepted McClellan's offer. In his autobiography McClellan described Custer as "a reckless, gallant boy, undeterred by fatigue, unconscious of fear and with a head that was always clear in danger. He said that Custer always brought him clear and intelligible reports of what he saw under the heaviest fire." McClellan, admittedly, became "much attached" to Custer.[5]

By 1863 Custer had risen to the rank of captain and was serving on the staff of General Alfred Pleasonton, Chief of Cavalry of the Army of the Potomac. Joseph Fought, who would serve with Custer throughout the Civil War, said that Pleasonton depended heavily on his staff officers—more so than on his brigade commanders. He said, if Captain Custer observed that it was important to make a movement or a charge, he would tell the brigade commander to do so and the brigade commander would comply because he knew that Pleasonton would confirm every one of Staff Officer Custer's instructions.[6]

Just prior to the battle at Gettysburg, Pleasonton was informed that three new brigades of cavalry were to be formed and he was to appoint three new brigadiers to lead them. Pleasonton selected three of his aides, Elon Farnsworth, Wesley Merritt and George Custer. It is often repeated that Custer received his brigadier general's star through an error by the War Department. This "fairy tail" had its origin in the Warner Brothers 1941 movie production, *They Died With Their Boots On*. Incredibly, some few years ago, this fiction was presented as fact in a New Jersey junior high school history textbook. Custer's promotion was indeed merited. It was officially endorsed in Special Orders No. 175, signed by order of General George Meade, commander of the Army of the Potomac, June 28, 1863. The order specifically listed the names of Farnsworth, Merritt and Custer.[7] Farnsworth would be killed at the Battle of Gettysburg less than a week after receiving his star. Merritt and Custer would survive Gettysburg and the war, and eventually distinguish themselves as division commanders.

Along with his brigadier general's star, Custer was given command of the Michigan Cavalry Brigade. Previous to Custer's promotion, it had become known to him that two regiments of cavalry were to be raised in Michigan. Custer had applied to Michigan's Governor Blair for a colonelcy in one of the regiments. Blair had turned him down. It was, indeed, ironic that Custer would now be given command of the entire Michigan Brigade. Judge Isaac Christiancy, a personal friend of Custer from Monroe, Michigan, remarked in a letter written to Custer soon after he had received his new command:

> How fortunate for you that Governor Blair had nothing for you. Every step of your remarkable advancement has been due to your own merit, without favor...often in the face of opposing influence, often of political origin.[8]

JUDGE I.T. CHRISTIANCY
Author's collection

The first major battle action Custer would see as leader of the Michigan Brigade occurred just five days after he received his promotion to brigadier. It was on the third and final day of the Battle of

Gettysburg that Custer would make his mark as a general of brigade. Confederate General Robert E. Lee envisioned breaking the stalemate at Gettysburg by a grand assault on the Union lines on Cemetery Ridge. Lee would send his great cavalry leader J.E.B. Stuart with six thousand Confederate Cavalrymen to attack the flank of the Union lines on Cemetery Ridge, while George Pickett's Division made a frontal assault. Lee's plan would end with the defeat of both Pickett's Division and Stuart's Cavalry.

Many students of the Battle have questioned Lee's wisdom in sending Pickett's Division against such a heavily defended position. Lee, however, was not a fool. He had planned an envelopment. (A simultaneous attack on the enemy's flank while assaulting its front.) Lee was not alone in knowing that an envelopement was the key to success in any frontal assault. All West Point cadets learned this tactic in their study of Napoleonic warfare taught at West Point. If Stuart had succeeded in the attempted envelopement, Pickett's charge would have succeeded, resulting in a Union defeat that could have prolonged the war for years. There is further evidence to convince that there may have been an envelopement planned. One of Stuart's staff officers, Henry B. McClellan tells us that Stuart himself ordered a single cannon to fire in four different directions sometime before the fight on the Rummel Farm, thus alerting every Federal in the area. If it was Stuart's intention to surprise the Federals, why did he order cannon fire that would certainly reveal his pressence. Could the cannon fire have been a signal to Lee that Stuart was in position to attempt the envelopement? Perhaps.[9]

Stuart's attempt to complete the envelopement was

thwarted, however by the newly appointed brigadier George Armstrong Custer and his Michigan Wolverines. The Second Cavalry Division was assigned to protect the flank of the Union Forces on Cemetery Ridge. Custer's brigade, attached to the Second Division, was posted just east of the division's main positions. As Stuart's cavalrymen moved toward Meade's flank they were discovered by Custer's Michigan Brigade pickets. Custer immediately requested permission to engage Stuart. Permission was granted. Custer met and defeated Stuart's famed Cavalry in a furious and decisive battle on the Rummel Farm, five miles east of Gettysburg. The battle on the Rummel Farm has been described as the last great horse to horse, man to man, saber to saber battle ever fought in the Western Hemisphere.[10] As a result of the action, Stuart retired from the field and a Union victory at Gettysburg was assured—as was a place in history for the youthful commander of the Michigan Brigade. A monument specifically honoring Custer and his Michigan Wolverines stands in a corn field on the outskirts of Gettysburg on what was the East Cavalry Battlefield. The inscription on the monument reads:

> This monument marks the field where the Michigan Brigade under it's gallant leader General George Custer, rendered signal and distinguished service in assisting to defeat the numerically superior force under the Confederate General J.E.B. Stuart who, in conjunction with Pickett's charge upon the center, attempted to turn the right flank of the Union Army at the critical hour of conflict on the afternoon of July 3rd, 1863.[11]

It is difficult to understand why so few Civil War historians place value on the cavalry fight east of Gettysburg. Perhaps it is because Lee never publically placed blame for the disastrous failure of Pickett's charge on Stuart's failure to complete the planned envelopment. Lee blamed only himself for the destruction of Pickett's Division. (George Pickett would go to his grave never forgiving Lee for the destruction of his gallant division at Gettysburg.) To understand the magnitude of Custer's accomplishment at the Rummel Farm, students of the battle can look to the unstinting praise he garnered from Union leaders after the Union victory at Gettysburg.

JAMES H. KIDD
Michigan Historical Collections

COL. JAMES H. KIDD
6TH MICHIGAN CAVALRY:

It was that battle (on the Rummel Farm) that gave great renown to the name of Custer as a general of brigade. It was that cavalry fight that saved Meade's right flank from being turned at the moment when Pickett made his famous assault upon the center on Cemetery Ridge. It was that fight that brought fame to the Michigan Brigade, all due to his matchless leadership and to his own prowess. It was that fight which but five days after the date of his commission, proved the wisdom of Custer's promotion from captain to brigade general.[12]

JUDSON KILPATRICK
National Archives

GENERAL JUDSON KILPATRICK,
COMMANDER OF THE THIRD CAVALRY DIVISION

To General Custer and his Brigade...all praise is due.[13]

DAVID M. GREGG
National Archives

GENERAL DAVID M. GREGG, COMMANDER OF THE 2ND CAVALRY DIVISION:

Brigadier General Custer, commanding Second Brigade, Third Division, very ably assisted me in the duties of my command.[14]

ALFRED PLEASONTON
National Archives

GENERAL ALFRED PLEASONTON, CHIEF OF CAVALRY:

Brigadier Generals Merritt and Custer, brigade commanders, have increased the confidence entertained in their ability and gallantry to lead troops on the field of battle.[15]

Custer would be cited for gallant and meritorious service for action at Gettysburg, Yellow Tavern, Winchester, Five Forks, Fisher's Hill and Appomatox. His complete Civil War service record, as listed in the Adjutant General's office at the War Department, is as follows:

Drilling volunteers at Washington, D.C., June to July 1861; in the Manassas Campaign of July, 1861, being engaged in the Battle of Bull Run, July 21, 1861; in the defenses of Washington, D.C., July to October 1861; absent sick, Oct. 1861 to Feb. 1862; in the Virginia Peninsular Campaign (Army of The Potomac), March to Aug. 1862, being in the Siege of Yorktown, Apr. 5 to May 4, 1862, and Aid-de-camp to Maj. Gen. McClellan in the Maryland Campaign, Sept. Oct. 1862, being engaged in the Battle of South Mountain, Sept. 14, 1862, Battle of Antietam, Sept. 17, 1862, and March to Warrenton Va. Oct. 1862; in the Rappahannock Campaign, (Army of the Potomac) March to June, 1863, being engaged in "Stoneman's Raid" towards Richmond, Apr. 13 to May 2, 1863, and combat of Brandy Station, as Aid-de-camp to General Pleasonton, June 9, 1863; in command of cavalry brigade (Army of The Potomac), in the Pennsylvania Campaign June-July 1863, being engaged in the action of Aldie, June 17, 1863, Battle of Gettysburg, July 3, 1863, and in various skirmishes in pursuit of the enemy to Warrentown, Va., July, 1863, with constant fighting at Monterey, July 4, Smithburg, July 5, Hagerstown, July 6, Williamsport, July 6, Boonsborough, July 8, Hagerstown, July 12, and Williamsport, July 14, 1863; in operations in central Virginia, Aug. 1863 to March 1864, being engaged in a skirmish at King George C.H., Aug. 24, 1863, action at Culpeper, Sept. 13, 1863, where he was wounded; Skirmish at Somerville Ford, Sept. 15, 1863, Reconnaissance to Liberty Mills, Sept 20-24, 1863, Action at James City, Oct. 10, and at Brandy Station, Oct.11, 1863, Movement to Centreville, Oct 12-18, 1863, actions at Gainsville, Oct. 19, and at Buckland's Mills, Oct 20, 1863, skirmish at Stevensburg, Nov. 8. 1863, and Mine Run Expedition, Nov. 26 to Dec. 3, 1863; on sick leave of absence March-April, 1864; in command of Brigade of Cavalry Corps (Army of The Potomac), in Richmond Campaign, Apr. 4 to Aug. 1, 1864, being engaged in the Battle of the Wilderness, May 6, 1864, Combat at Todd's Tavern, May 7, 1864, raid to Haxall's Landing, and returning to New Castle, May 9-29, 1864, Battle of Yellow Tavern, May 11, 1864, Combat of Meadow Bridge, May 12, 1864, action at Hanovertown, May 27, 1864, Battle of Hawes's Shop, May 28, 1864, Battle of Cold Harbor, May 31 to June 1, 1864, Battle of Trevillian

Station, June 11, 1864, and skirmish at Newark, June 12, 1864; in command of brigade, Aug. 4 to Sept. 26, 1864, and 3rd Division, Oct 2, 1864, to March 26, 1865, Cavalry Corps, in Shenandoah Campaign, being engaged in Skirmishes near Winchester, Aug. 12, Front Royal, Aug. 16, Shephards, Aug 25, Smithfield, Aug. 28, and Opequan Creek, Sept. 15, 1864, Battle at Opequan, Sept. 19, 1864, Actions at Cedarville, Sept. 23, Luray, Sept.24, Columbia Furnace, Oct. 7 and at Tom's Run, Oct. 9, 1864, Battle of Cedar Creek, Oct 19, 1864, actions of Middletown, Nov. 12, and Lacey Springs (in command) Mar. 2, 1865; in command of Cavalry Division, Mar. 26 to May 29, 1865, being engaged in the Battle of Dinwidde C. H., March 31, 1865, Battle of Five Forks, Apr. 1, 1865, Battle of Sailor's Creek, Apr. 6, 1865, Action at Appomattox Station, Apr. 8, 1865, Capitulation of General Lee at Appomattox C.H., Apr. 9, 1865.[16]

PHILIP
SHERIDAN
National Archives

In recognition of Custer's outstanding service to the Nation, General Philip Sheridan, at the conclusion of the surrender ceremonies at Appomattox, purchased the table on which the instrument of surrender was drawn from Wilber McLean for twenty dollars in gold and sent it to Elizabeth Custer with the following message:

My dear Madam - I respectfully present to you the small table on which the conditions for the surrender of the Confederate Army of Northern Virginia were written by Lt. General Grant—permit me to say, Madam, that there is scarcely an individual in our service who has contributed more to bring this about than your gallant husband.[17]

The table, along with the white flag of surrender accepted by Custer at Appomatox, resides in the Smithsonian Institute in Washington, D.C., the gift of Elizabeth Bacon Custer.

CHAPTER TWO
Epilogue

STEVEN M. GAINES

14th Virginia Cavalry

> Of the cavalry leaders on the Union side I can
> speak with special confiedence, having met
> them in more than a hundered fights, and I do
> not hesitate to say that, in skill and boldness,
> not one was the equal of General Custer.

The above may be found in a letter from Steven Gaines to
Elizabeth Custer dated Novemebr 12, 1906. The letter is
in the Elizabeth Custer Collection, Little Big Horn
National Monument, Crow Agency, Montana.

CAPTAIN S. H. BALLARD

6th Michigan Cavalry

> When Custer made a charge he was the first
> sabre that struck, for he was always ahead.

From the Grand Rapids [Michigan] Daily Eagle, July 8,
1876.

MAJOR G. D. HAMILTON

8th New York Cavalry

> In my opinion, Custer was the best cavalry
> General in the army.

The above was taken from a letter from G. D. Hamilton to

Elizabeth Custer dated April 9, 1902. The letter is in the Elizabeth Custer Collection, Little Big Horn National Monument, Crow Agency, Montana.

TULLY MCCREA

McCrea was a classmate of George Custer at West Point.

> Custer could always make the battlefield glamorous and the soldier's profession the noblest pursuit of life.

This quote may be found in Catherine S. Crary's *Dear Belle*, Wesleyan University Press, Middletown, Connecticut. P. 108

GENERAL PHILIP H. SHERIDAN

General Sheridan commanded the Cavalry Corps Army of the Potomac. He here describes the action at the great cavalry fight at Yellow Tavern where the indomitable Confederate cavalry leader J.E.B. Stuart was mortally wounded.

> ...the enemy, desperate but still confident, poured in a heavy fire from his line and from a battery which enfiladed the Brook road, and made Yellow Tavern an uncomfortably hot place. Gibb's and Devin's brigades, however, held fast there, while Custer, supported by Chapman's brigade, attacked the enemies left and battery in a mounted charge.

> Custer's charge, with Chapman on his flank and the rest of Wilson's Division sustaining him was brilliantly executed. Beginning at a walk, he increased his gait to a trot, and then at full speed rushed the enemy.

After Custer's charge, the Confederate Cavalry was badly broken up, the main portion of it being driven in a route toward Ashland and a small part in the direction of Richmond.

The above quotes may be found in The Personal Memories of P. H. Sheridan, Vol. 1, New York, Charles Webster and Co., 1888, P.P 374-375.

The Years on the Plains

There is little doubt that Philip H. Sheridan had great admiration for Custer and felt he owed much to him for his own success in the Shenendoah. His sentiments were clearly expressed in a letter of recommendation written to Secretary of War Edwin M. Stanton upon the reorganization of the army after the Civil War had concluded:

> Sir, I have the honor to make application for the appointment of Brevet Brigadier (sic) General G.A. Custer, U.S.A. to be Colonel of Cavalry upon reorganization of the army. The record of this officer is so conspicuous as to render its recital by me unnecessary. I ask this appointment as a reward to one of the most gallant and efficient officers that ever served under me.[1]

In the postwar army, Custer was appointed Lt. Colonel of Cavalry and was assigned to the newly formed United States 7th Cavalry. The colonel commanding, A.J. Smith, was continually assigned to other duties thereby leaving Custer in command of the regiment.

Kathrine Gibson, wife of Captain Francis Gibson, an officer in the 7th Cavalry, wrote in her diary:

> General Custer's outstanding personality made such an imprint on his fellow Officers that this organization was known, and always will be, as Custer's 7th.[2]

The Seventh saw little action against Indians during Custer's early command days. Its activities were confined to patrolling and chasing Indians. There was little direct contact with them.

It was while campaigning in Kansas in 1867 that Custer created serious problems for himself. He made the arbitrary decision to absent himself from his command and visit his wife at Fort Riley. For this unauthorized absence and for other serious infractions, charges were preferred against him. He was accused of absenting himself from his command without proper authority, unauthorized use of Government vehicles, and ordering deserters hunted down and brought back to the command dead or alive. Custer was convicted of all charges and sentenced to one year suspension from rank and pay. The lenient sentence was no doubt handed down in consideration of Custer's outstanding Civil War record. He went home to Monroe, Michigan to wait out the suspension.

It was also during this early post-Civil War period that Custer began to acquire a reputation as a martinet. Several subordinate officers attested to Custer's unusually harsh treatment of troublesome soldiers. It is difficult to understand what was behind Custer's command behavior at this stage of his life. It seems that he simply was unable to adjust to the drastic changes in his career. With the Civil War concluded and the army reduced in size, many career officers were reduced in rank and pay, the twenty-seven year old Custer from the lofty position of Major General of Volunteers to Lieutenant Colonel. He was now commanding a regiment of cavalry on a lonely frontier post instead of enjoying his famed role as commander of the Third Cavalry Division fighting to preserve the Union. He was no longer being lionized almost daily for his achievements.

Examining the very serious charge of ordering deserters hunted down and returned to the command dead or alive, the following should be considered. Custer was dealing with a different type of soldier in the postwar army than the one he had commanded in the Civil War. In the war of southern rebellion, Custer led soldiers dedicated to the cause they were fighting for. Discipline was not a major problem. In the peacetime army, however, it was a different story. Except for a few career men, the post-Civil War army was generally made up of misfits. The army was often a haven for men who found it difficult to cope with civilian life and for opportununists who sought refuge from the law for one offense or another. Newly arrived European immigrants, struggling with a new language, joined the army as a way of becoming assimilated. And then there were infamous "Snowbirds." Snowbird was the name attached to those who would join the army in winter wanting a free ticket west, and then at the first sign of spring desert to the gold fields. They were many and created a serious problem in the western regiments. Western field commanders could not afford—nor could they allow—wholesale depletion of their ranks through desertions. At the time Custer ordered deserters brought back dead or alive, the 7th Cavalry was operating in enemy territory. Deserters were seriously thinning the regiment's ranks, thereby putting their fellow soldiers lives in jeopardy. It has been argued that Custer, being in a combat situation, had the right to give such an order.

In late summer and early fall of 1868, the settlers on the borders of Kansas and Colorado had suffered losses of 117 killed, 16 wounded, four women and two children captured and numerous horses, mules and cattle stolen during Indian raids. General Sheridan planned to stop these raids by initiating a winter campaign against the Indians of the southern plains. He wanted Custer to lead it. He wired Washington requesting Custer's sentence be remitted. He also sent Custer the following wire:

> Generals Sherman, Sully and myself and near-
> ly all the officers of your regiment have asked
> for you, and I hope the application (for remit-
> tance of sentence) will be successful. Can you
> come at once?[3]

Sheridan's request for the remittance of Custer's sentence was favorably received and Custer immediately rejoined his regiment. Francis M. Gibson, an officer of the regiment, said that Custer's arrival seemed to infuse new life in the command. He said the 7th had unconsciously fallen into a state of inertia, and with Custer's coming, action, purpose, energy and general strengthening of the loose joints was the order of the day.[4]

Custer led the 7th Cavalry in Sheridan's winter campaign against the Southern Cheyenne. He found Black Kettle's village on the banks of the Washita River and destroyed it. One hundred and three warriors were killed in the fight and fifty three women and children were brought back by the returning troops. Despite orders by Custer that no women or children should be harmed in the attack, causalities were inescapable. It would have been a miracle if there were none. Despite outcries from the Indian Bureau that Black Kettle's band was peaceful, evidence proved the opposite was true. There were several white captives in the village. A small white boy was brutally slain by an Indian woman as he was about to be rescued by 7th Cavalry troopers. Immediately after killing the boy, she was shot and killed by Captain Frederick Benteen.[5] The mail pouch of a pony expressman, who had been recently killed, was found in the village. If Black Kettle's village was peaceful, then his camp was a gathering place for young Cheyenne raiders. Black Kettle's sister was one of the fifty three captives brought back to Camp Supply, and her story was that she had constantly asked Black Kettle to stop the raids on the white settlements.

The 7th Cavalry did not escape the Battle of the Washita unscathed. Among the dead and wounded was Captain Louis Hamilton, grandson of Alexander Hamilton. Hamilton was killed in the initial charge. Major Joel Elliott and eighteen enlisted men were killed when, against orders, they pursued a group of Indians fleeing the village. Captain Barnitz, who was with Custer at Appomattox, was "gut shot" and assumed mortally wounded; somehow he survived. Barnitz was one of the 7th Cavalry officers who was very critical of Custer prior to the Washita fight, but there was no further criticism of Custer by Barnitz after he was brought back from the battlefield alive.

The Battle of the Washita was controversial then and remains so today. Sheridan and the people on the frontier, however, were relieved after the defeat of the Indians at the Washita. It put an end to the killing and raiding along the Smokey Hill Trail. After the campaign, Custer received the following message from General Sheridan:

> I am very much rejoiced at the success of your expedition, and feel very proud of our winter operations, and of the Officers and men who bore the privations so manfully. The energy and rapidity shown during one of the heaviest snow storms known to this section of the country, with the temperature below freezing, the gallantry and bravery displayed, resulting in such signal success, reflects credit on the 7th Cavalry...and the Major General commanding expresses his thanks to the officers and men engaged in the Battle of the Washita, and special congratulations to their distinguished Commander Brevet Major General George A. Custer [Sheridan here identifies Custer by his Civil War rank] for the efficient and gallant service opening the campaign against the hostile Indians north of the Arkansas.[6]

Following the Washita campaign, relative peace reigned on the frontier. The Indian situation quieted down and there was little for the 7th Cavalry to do. Custer and his command were dispersed with individual companies seeing service in different parts of the southern section of the United States.

In 1873, one of the prevailing philosophies throughout the Country was that of Manifest Destiny. It was strongly believed that God had given all of the land between the two great oceans to the white race to do with it as it saw fit. If any obstacles, including the Indians, got in the way of progress, they were to be overcome by any possible means. Americans believed that their Country was destined to stretch "from sea to shining sea." The railroads were inching across the Country to eventually link the twogreat oceans. The Northern Pacific, one of the railroad giants, was starting to push into the Yellowstone River Country...territory that was still relatively unknown to the white man. It just so happened that the area was part of the Plains Indians' last great hunting grounds; they would, it was discovered, fight for it.

Custer and the 7th Cavalry were reunited at this time and ordered to take station at Fort Abraham Lincoln and other forts along the Missouri River in Dakota Territory. The 7th's first assignment was to protect the Northern Pacific surveying crews as they headed West into Indian Country in the summer of 1873. On that expedition, there were two skirmishs with Indians along the Yellowstone River, but neither was of major consequence.

In 1874, Custer and his 7th Cavalry were ordered into the Black Hills to map the area and look for possible sites for future roads and military forts. Broadly interpreted, the treaty of Laramie (signed by the Sioux in 1868) can be said to have granted the government such privilege, the Sioux however considered it a wrongful invasion of their land. Land that had been granted them by treaty was now being "visited" by the white man, and the Indian knew that where one white man went, other white men would surely follow. Geologists accompanying the expedition found small quantities of gold in the Black Hills, and when the word got out, the stampede was on. The army at first tried to keep the prospectors out of the Hills, but it was hopeless. When miners were stopped at one entrance, they merely backed off and went in another way. Knowing they were locked into a futile situation, the Government offered to buy the Black Hills from the Sioux. But the area was sacred to the Indians and not for sale at any price. The Government's decision to enter the Hills set the stage for the final chapter in free Indian history: the end of his way of life and his eventual confinement to the reservation.

After General Custer's death at the Little Big Horn, his wife Elizabeth had some very interesting things to say about her husband's relations with the Indians and the Black Hills:

ELIZABETH CUSTER
Author's collection

I well remember how the great chiefs of the Sioux came frequently to General Custer's quarters at Fort Lincoln and held long conferences with him about the Black Hills. They urged that the white man should not go into the Hills, that it was dangerous and would bring war. The Indian deeply cherished the Black Hills. The country was different from the dry plains and the bad lands because there was timber there and water and wonderful hunting. The Chiefs said that their people would fight to keep the land that was promised to them. The Indian despised the men who spoke with forked tongues, or broke promises, and after they were gone the General would say the Government must keep its promise to the Indian. These Indian conferences were always given complete right of way by the General and the greatest respect and deference was shown to the Chiefs. The General always gave a feast for them afterwards. He recognized a true nobility in the Indian character, and respected their feelings of attachment to the land. There was a time after the battle of the Little Big Horn when I could not have said this, but as years have passed I have become convinced that the Indians were deeply wronged.[8]

Elsewhere she is found to have said:

His [Custer's] intercourse with them led him to conclude that if he were an Indian he would prefer to cast his lot among those of my people who adhered to the free open plains rather than submit to the confined limits of a reservation there to be the recipient of the blessed benefits of civilization with its vices thrown in without stint [9]

CHAPTER THREE
Epilogue

ANNIE YATES

Annie Yates was the widow of Captain George Yates who commanded F Troop United States 7th Cavalry at the Battle of The Little Big Horn. He died with Custer at the last stand.

ANNIE YATES

Brian C. Pohanka
Collection

Custer's Logical Mind

Custer's face was not the face of a thoughtless, impulsive man, it was the somewhat worn, but eager continence of a man who had faced extraordinary responsibilities in youth; his eye was penetrating, his broad massive brow was the brow of a thinker not one who would rush into danger simply for the glory of it. Custer talked very fast in a nervous, energetic way and the fact that his face was mobile and expressive may have given to strangers the impression that he was impulsive. He was a rapid reasoner and in a few moments grasped a situation...and acted upon it. His logic was instant, the results being obtained so quickly as to probably give the impression of rashness to those who did not know him.

The above, undated piece, written by Annie Yates, may be found in the Elizabeth Custer Collection, Little Big Horn National Monument, Crow Agency, Montana. sec. C -19 C-2889

GENERAL THOMAS ROSSER, C.S.A.

Rosser was a classmate of George Custer at West Point. He left the Military Academy before graduation to return to his native state of Virginia to fight for the Confederacy. He remained a close friend of Custer even though they met on opposing battlefields during the Civil War. Rosser later served as a civil engineer for the Northern Pacific Railroad and was on the Yellowstone Expedition of 1873. The 7th Cavalry was assigned that summer to escorted the survey crews as they plotted the railroad's route west thereby reuniting Custer and Rosser.

The time I would rather have had a picture of George was on the Yellowstone campaign. George sat on his horse out in advance, calmly looking the Indians over, full of suppressed excitement, but with calculating judgement and strength of purpose in his face. I thought him then one of the finest specimens of a soldier I had ever seen.

The Army and Navy Journal, July 22, 1876.

CUSTER (foreground) RELAXING WITH OTHER YOUNG CIVIL WAR OFFICERS.

CUSTER'S SECRETARY AT FORT LINCOLN, RICHARD ROBERTS, SAID OF
CUSTER'S CLOSE RELATIONSHIP WITH HIS ANIMALS:
"ANIMALS, LIKE CHILDREN, SELDOM ERR."

The Road to the Little Big Horn

By 1876, the year of the battle of The Little Big Horn, most Indians had reluctantly accepted reservation life. There were those, however, who rigorously opposed it and would not submit. Among them was the Sioux Chief Sitting Bull, an inspirational and spiritual leader of his people. Those who chose to stay away from the reservations, were often joined in summer by "reservation Indians" who wished to hunt for meat for their poorly fed families and to enjoy the pleasures of the old life that were quickly fading away.

In 1875, the Federal Government made the decision that all Indians were to be confined on reservations. None would be allowed to enjoy the free, roaming life they had lived for centuries on the open plains. Runners were sent out to inform the tribes that they had to come in to reservations by January 31, 1876 or they would be considered hostile and be brought in by force. The ultimatum was largely ignored and the matter was turned over to the War Department for military action. The War department drafted a plan: Three columns would move into the Big Horn Country where the roaming bands were known to be. General George Crook would bring a column north from Fort Fetterman in Southern Wyoming, Colonel John Gibbon would lead troops east from Fort Shaw in South Central Montana, and Lt.

Colonel George Armstrong Custer and his fabled United States 7th Cavalry would come west from Fort Abraham Lincoln in Dakota Territory. Although the three columns would converge on the same area, there was no plan for the columns to operate together. Each column was considered strong enough to handle any situation it would encounter.

While the 7th was preparing for the 1876 campaign, Custer inadvertently caused the displeasure of the President of the United States. The impeachment of President Ulysses S. Grant's Secretary of War, General William Belknap, was being sought by the Congress of the United States. A House committee was charging not only Belknap but the President's brother Orville Grant with illegally selling government post traderships in the West for illegal fees and kickbacks. (Post traderships were authorized and proprietors appointed by the Secretary of War to provide trading at frontier military posts too far removed from towns or cities.) There had obviously been serious malfeasance, and knowing Custer as a critic of the administration in this area, the committee subpoenaed him. Custer first requested that he be allowed to testify by questionnaire. Later he decided that he should appear. Reluctantly, he left Fort Lincoln to attend the hearings in Washington. His testimony, however, amounted to mere hearsay, and, realizing this, the young general requested that he be excused so that he could return to his post on the frontier and resume preparations for the coming campaign. His request was granted. But Custer's problems had only begun.

It was customary, at that time, for all army officers, when visiting Washington, to pay a visit to the President of the United States or the Commander-in-Chief of Army before leaving the city to return to their posts. After he was released by the Committee, Custer, following protocol, went to see the President. Grant refused to see him. Custer had incurred his wrath by his testimony at the impeachment proceedings. The President felt that Custer had maligned him and his administration. Furthermore, he had taken Custer's testimony as a personal affront since it involved his brother Orville. Custer realized it was hopeless to placate the President, so he went to see the Commanding General William Sherman. Unfortunately Sherman was not in Washington. Completely frustrated by events and anxious to return to his regiment, Custer left his card for Sherman with a message that he had been there to pay his respects and was now returning to his command. Custer then left Washington for Fort Lincoln.

President Grant saw his chance for revenge. No matter what the circumstance, Custer had left Washington without seeing him or the Army's Commanding General. When Custer's westbound train arrived in Chicago, he was placed under arrest and informed that he could not accompany his regiment on the coming campaign. Nonetheless, Custer received permission to continue on to St. Paul, where on arrival he sought the intercession of his Civil War mentor General Philip Sheridan and the Departmental Commander General Alfred Terry. He felt certain Sheridan would not let him down, since they had been through so much together during the late war. Of Terry's support he was confident from the words of a letter he had received just before leaving Fort Lincoln to testify at the Belknap hearings. Wrote Terry, "Your services are indispensable and no thought of transfer can be entertained."[1]

Both Terry and Sheridan sent messages to the President asking for Custer's reinstatement. Both stated Custer's services would be invaluable to the success of the campaign. Custer also received help from the New York Herald whose publisher, James Gordon Bennett, was a personal friend and admirer. The Herald had picked up the story of Custer's arrest and was blasting the President with headlines such as, "Is this how every person who exposes Grant's corrupt administration be dealt with?"[2]

President Grant gave in under the pressure and restored Custer to his command. However, Grant ordered that Custer was to go only in command of his regiment, the Departmental Commander General Terry was to accompany the expedition and be in over-all command.

———

As early as March of 1876 there had been action in the Indian Country, when an element of Crook's command engaged with a Cheyenne village along the Powder River. On June 17, 1876, just eight days before Custer would be defeated at the Little Big Horn, Crook's entire command would meet the Sioux and Northern Cheyenne in a pitched battle at the Rosebud River. The battle would be indecisive, however, Crook, with more than twice the men Custer had under his command, felt it necessary to retreat to his base camp on Goose Creek in north central Wyoming Territory.

From Goose Creek, Crook sent a message back to the States, asking for more men and supplies. Yet, aware that two other columns were operating in the area and knowing their approximate location, Crook made no attempt to get word to either advising them on the formidable numbers of Indians he had encountered at the Rosebud. True, he was not obliged to cooperate with the other columns, and it would have been difficult for a messenger to get through as the area was teeming with hostiles, still an attempt might have been made. A seasoned scout moving well to the east and then north could have easily picked up Terry and Custer's trail. He may not have reached Terry in time, but at least an attempt would have been made.

As it was, Terry would come by intelligence about an Indian encampment along the lower Rosebud on his own; it would not, however, convey to Terry the present location of the Indians or the sense of numbers Crook had met on the Rosebud. Gibbon and Terry had joined forces on the Yellowstone, seeking the Sioux so they could move against them. In late May, before joining with Terry, Colonel Gibbon's scouts had discovered a large Indian encampment on the Rosebud River. Terry was advised of the encampment after Gibbon and he joined forces.

Before sending forces against the camp, Terry wanted to make sure the camp had not moved to the east. He ordered the 7th Cavalry's second in command, Major Marcus A. Reno, with six companies of the 7th, to scout the area east of the Rosebud. Terry was quite sure Reno would find no sign of Indians, but wanted to be absolutely certain the Indians had not wandered in that direction. Reno was ordered not to go near the Rosebud. Terry knew that Indians had been there and if they were still in the area, he did not want them flushed out. Reno was given Mitch Bouyer, one of Gibbon's best scouts, to guide the column. Bouyer, a Canadian mixed blood, had spent time with Sitting Bull and his Sioux and knew the area well.

Finding no sign of Indians east of the Rosebud Valley, Reno, instead of covering all the area he was ordered to scout, headed straight for the Rosebud. One can guess, that Mitch Bouyer, having been with the scouting party that had earlier discovered the Indian camp on the Rosebud, told Reno that if he wanted to see Indians he could show him where there were plenty. When Reno arrived at the Rosebud, he found a large lodge pole trail heading south. Reno followed the trail for a time and then, running short of supplies, turned his column north and returned to the base camp on the Yellowstone to report to General Terry.

When Reno made his report, Terry was furious with the 7th's Junior Major for disobeying his orders. He probably would have preferred charges against Reno after the campaign had ended if the results had been different. Be that as it may, Terry now had something to go by. The Indians they were seeking were still on the Rosebud, but had moved south. They would either be camped further up that stream or on the next stream west, the Little Big Horn. With the general location of the Indians now known, Terry, Gibbon and Custer held a council of war on the river steamer Far West.

The Far West had been pushed up the Yellowstone with supplies under the able command of Grant Marsh, one of the best river boat captains on the Missouri. It was decided that Custer would take his 7th Cavalry up the Rosebud Valley following the trail discovered by Major Reno.

Terry and Gibbon would take Gibbon's Command and the balance of Terry's up the Yellowstone by steamer to the mouth of the Big Horn River and then march up that stream into the valley of the Little Big Horn. It was thought that if the Indians were camped on the Little Big Horn River they could be caught between the two columns. No specific plan of attack, however, was ever agreed upon between Terry and Custer. Lt. James Bradley, Colonel Gibbon's Chief of Scouts, said that it was understood that if Custer found the Indians he was at liberty to attack at once. Bradley said that he felt sure it would be Custer alone who would be in at the kill.[3] Custer received his written instructions from Terry and left the Yellowstone on the morning of June 22nd, three days before he would make his last stand at the Little Big Horn.

Terry had made it clear to Custer that he and Gibbon could not be in the Little Big Horn Valley until the 26th of June. Custer has been generally condemned for attacking the village on the Little Big Horn on the 25th of June, instead of waiting until Terry's estimated arrival date of the 26th. This 25th attack date and 26th arrival date has fueled the charge that Custer intentionally arrived at the battlefield a day earlier than planned so that he could gather all the laurels for himself and his command. The charge is easily refuted. No one in either command knew exactly where the Indians would be found. If they were in the Little Big Horn Valley it would have been impossible to know exactly where. Even if the exact location had been known, how could anyone expect two commands, traveling by different routes, to arrive at the same place at the same time, especially traveling in unknown country? In fact Terry and Gibbon did not arrive at the Custer battle site until the 27th of June. If Custer had waited until the 26th he still would have faced the Indians alone.

In order to consider any charge of disobedience against Custer one must first read Terry's orders to him. The orders, therefore, are reproduced here exactly as they were written:

> *Camp at the Mouth of the Rosebud River, Montana, Territory, June, 22nd, 1876.*
>
> Lieut. Col. Custer, 7th Cavalry
>
> Colonel:
> The Brigadier-General commanding directs that, as soon as your regiment can be made ready for the march, you will proceed up the Rosebud in pursuit of the Indians whose trail was discovered by Major Reno a few days since. *It is, of course, impossible to give you any definite instructions in regard to this movement, and were it not impossible for me to do so, the Department commander places too much confidences in your zeal, energy and ability to wish to impose upon you precise orders which might hamper your actions when nearly in contact with the enemy. He will, however, indicate to you his own views of what your action should be, and he desires that you should conform to them unless you shall see sufficient reason for departing from them.*He thinks you should proceed up the Rosebud until you ascertain definitely the direction in which the trail above spoken leads. Should it be found (as it appears almost certain that it will be found) to turn towards the Little Horn, he thinks that you still should proceed southward, perhaps as far as the headwaters of the Tongue, and then

turn toward the Little Horn, feeling constantly, however, to your left, so as to preclude the
possibility of the escape of the Indians to the
south or southeast by passing around your left
flank. The column of Colonel Gibbon is now
in motion for the mouth of the Big Horn. As
soon as it reaches that point it will cross the
Yellowstone and move up at least as far as the
forks of the Big and Little Horns. Of course its
future movements must be controlled by circumstances as they arise, but it is hoped that
the Indians, if upon the Little Horn, may be so
nearly enclosed by the two columns that their
escape will be impossible.

The Departmental Commander
desires that on your way up the Rosebud you
should thoroughly examine the upper part of
Tullock's Creek, and that you should endeavor
to send a scout through to Colonel Gibbon's
column, with information of the result of your
examination. The lower part of the creek will
be examined by a detachment of Colonel
Gibbon's command. The supply steamer will
be pushed up the Big Horn as far as the forks if
the river is found navigable for that distance,
and the Departmental Commander, who will
accompany the column of Colonel Gibbon,
desires that you report to him there not later
than the expiration of the time for which you
have been rationed, unless in the meantime
you receive further orders.

Very Respectfully,
Your obedient servant,
E.W. Smith, Captain, 18th Infantry
Acting Assistant Adjutant-General[4]

<small>(italics by author)</small>

The orders gave Custer the greatest of latitude. The *sufficient reason or reasons* referred to in Terry's orders must have been thoroughly discussed during the council of war held on the Far West the night before Terry wrote his letter of instructions to Custer. The contingencies that were discussed were perhaps too numerous to include in the orders and so were covered by the phrase *sufficient reason*.

Terry's orders also instructed Custer to report to him no later than the time he had been rationed for, and Custer was rationed for fifteen days. Since the orders were dated June 22, Terry evidently concluded that there was a possibility that he would not see or hear from Custer until the 7th of July. Custer advised his officers to have their men carry extra salt on the scout, as he intended to follow the Indian trail even if it led to the agencies in Nebraska. If it did, he said, the command might have to resort to eating mule meat. Custer was, in fact, prepared for a long scout and was far from having a race for glory in mind. His instructions to his officers clearly shows he was concerned about running past the fifteen day contingency.

Custer left the camp on the Yellowstone on June 22nd. He picked up the Indian trail reported by Major Reno and followed it up the Rosebud. As the trail led south it became fresher and fresher. The entire command became aware that the Indians could not be far ahead. After two days the trail turned westward as Terry predicted it would. Custer now had a decision to make. Terry had given him the option to deviate from his written orders if he had sufficient reason to do so. Custer made the decision to stay on the Indian trail. Was there sufficient reason?

Custer was on an extremely fresh trail, so fresh that by abandoning it he would have betrayed all that he knew about Indian fighting. Every experienced officer on the frontier knew that when Indians discovered troops in the proximity of their village they would pull up stakes and run: They would not fight in their villages unless forced to do so. Indians preferred to fight outside their village, thereby keeping their families out of harm's way. The only way, therefore, to capture an Indian village was to surprise it. The only way to surprise it was to move quickly, to doggedly stay with it until "there." General Sherman in a letter written one month after the battle to Senator I.T. Christiancy said:

> In all our former experience in that region, and in similar cases, success was only possible by rapid movement, so as to catch the warrior whilst encumbered with lodges and families.[5]

WILLIAM T.
SHERMAN
National Archives

Terry had given Custer additional latitude when he said in his orders: "the Departmental Commander places too much confidence in your zeal, energy, and ability to wish to impose upon you precise orders which might hamper your action when nearly in contact with the enemy." Was Custer nearly in contact with the enemy? Only he could make that decision considering the circumstances that existed. Post-battle information cannot be considered in judging Custer's decision to stay with the Indian trail. If a court-martial had been convened to decide whether or not Custer had disobeyed Terry's orders, it is difficult to conceive of a conviction when comparing Custer's actions with Terry's orders. Custer felt he was very close to the village and did not want to give up the chance of a successful engagement. If the trail had not been fresh, there would have been no urgency and Custer probably would have gone further south as Terry had suggested. If Custer had decided on that option, regardless of the circumstances that confronted him, Terry, perhaps, would have been in serious trouble. He, not Custer, would have been the one who arrived first at the Sioux Village on the Little Big Horn and would have had to battle alone the same Indians who destroyed Custer. Had that been the case, Terry might not have fared as badly as Custer since he commanded mostly infantry and Indians did not like to fight "the walking soldiers." (They would usually go out of their way to avoid contact with them.) The campaign would have fallen flat, and Terry would have shouldered the blame for ordering Custer out of supporting distance.

With the decision made to stay on the trail, Custer led his troopers west on a night march toward the Divide that separated the Rosebud and Little Big Horn Valleys. The pitch black night made it difficult for the men to stay in column. Most of the troopers kept banging their tin drinking cups against metal objects on their saddles so the trooper behind could follow the sound. The column was finally halted while still on the eastern side of the divide. Custer's reason for the night march was to get his cavalry as close to the Indian encampment as possible under the cover of darkness. Once on the Divide, he planned to conceal his troops in the mountains and then plan for a dawn attack on the 26th, the day of Terry's estimated arrival in the Little Big Horn Valley. A dawn attack had been successful for Custer at the Washita fight in 1868. It was logical that he would again attempt to use that tactic.

While back on the Rosebud, Custer had been informed by his Crow Indian scouts that there was a promontory on the Divide called the Crows Nest. The vantage point was fifteen miles distant from the Little Big Horn River. Custer was told that from there, the valley of the Little Big Horn could be seen. Custer sent his Chief of Scouts Lt. Charles Varnum ahead with "his Indians" to see what could be seen from the observation point reported by the Crows. Varnum and the scouts arrived at the Crows Nest well before dawn. Varnum curled up on the ground in an attempt to get some much needed sleep. His eyes burned and his body ached from long hours in the saddle. At first light the scouts awakened Varnum and told him that a pall of smoke hung over the Little Big Horn Valley. They also told him they could see an enormous pony herd grazing on the benchland west of the river. Varnum was told if he wanted to see the herd, he should look for worms crawling in the grass. Though Varnum could not see all the Indian scouts said they had seen, he sent a message back to Custer reporting what the scouts had told him. After receiving Varnum's message, Custer ordered the command to stay where it was while he went ahead to the vantage point to see for himself.

When Custer arrived at the Crows Nest, conditions were a little different than they had been earlier that morning. The sun was higher in the sky, causing heat waves to reflect off the parched Montana countryside. Therefore, Custer could not see what his scouts had seen earlier. While at the Crows Nest, the scouts told Custer they had spotted Indians close to the Divide. They added that the Indians were circling their ponies as they rode west back toward their village. This was their way of signaling danger. Custer was also told that a few of his scouts had gone after the circling Indians in an attempt to prevent them from reaching the village. Custer and his Indians scouts then had a heated disagreement, the scouts insisting the column had been discovered and Custer arguing that it had not.

Custer left the Crows Nest to return to his command not completely sure of what lay ahead. As he approached the command, it was moving slowly forward. His brother Captain Thomas Custer and his brother-in-law Lt. James Calhoun were riding out ahead of the column. Custer charged toward them demanding to know who the devil had ordered the column to move when he had left orders for the column to stay where it was. Tom replied that he did not know. Custer's anger at this disobedience indicates that it was still his intention to keep the column concealed in the mountains and make preparations for a dawn attack the following day. What happened next, however, convinced Custer his scouts had been right, the Indians were aware of his presence and the advance of his column was—if accidentally—the right move.

Tom Custer informed his brother that one of the mules had lost a pack somewhere on the back trail and that Sergeant Curtis and several men had been sent back to retrieve it. The detail had found the pack all right, Tom went on, but they also found a small party of Indians attempting to open same. Curtis and his men had opened fire on the Indians and they abandoned the pack in a hurry. This event finally convinced Custer that the command had been discovered.

Custer immediately called his officers together to discuss the situation. All at the conference agreed that the column probably had been discovered and the only avenue open to them now was to get down to the valley as quickly as possible and attempt to capture the village before it scattered. Familiar with Indian proclivities, each officer believed that the Indians would not stand and fight but would attempt to escape from the advancing column.

The officers returned to their commands and Custer signaled the column forward. After crossing the Divide, he and his Adjutant Lt. William Winer Cooke went off to the side of the trail, dismounted and discussed the division of the regiment. When they returned to the column, Captain Frederick Benteen was assigned companies D, H and K, and ordered to advance toward the Little Big Horn Valley at an oblique angle to the southwest and to keep going until he could see into the Valley. If he found Indians along the way he was to pitch into them and send word back to the main column. Once Benteen was sure there were no Indians to the south, he was to return to the trail and follow after the command. Major Marcus Reno was given command of companies M, A and G, and ordered to advance down the left bank of a small mountain stream that flowed west toward the valley floor. (The mountain stream would, from that day on, be identified as Reno Creek.) Custer kept companies, C, F, E, I and L under his immediate command. Both Custer and Reno's Companies would advance down Reno Creek paralleling each other, Reno on the south side of the creek and Custer on the north. Captain Thomas McDougal was left behind with his Company B to escort the Pack Train. Six troopers from each of the advancing companies were detached and left with the train to help control the fractious mules. The train itself would be commanded by Lt. Edward Mathey. McDougal was instructed to give the command a twenty minute head start and then follow after. And so the entire command was set in motion on what was to be a reconnaissance in force.

CHAPTER FOUR
Epilogue

BLOODY KNIFE

Bloody Knife was Custer's favorite Indian scout. He was killed while serving with Major Marcus Reno's detachment at the Battle of the Little Big Horn.

> No other man could ride all day and never sleep.

Bloody Knife made the above statement during the Black Hills Expedition in 1874. It may be found in Frederick S. Dellenbach's *George Armstrong Custer* York, MacMillan &Co., 1917 P.P. 1-2.

PRIVATE JOHN BURKMAN

A Troop,, 7th Cavalry

Burkman served as General Custer's orderly for nine years. There can be little doubt that he knew Custer as well as any enlisted man in the 7th Cavalry.

> The General was all soldier. I've heerd folks sayin' Custer rushed into things headlong, specially in that last campaign on the Little Big Horn. That ain't true. Thar never was a man took things more serious. Thar never was a man worked harder than he did those last few weeks. Why, he cared fur us men o' the Seventh. He was brave hisself. He expected us to be brave. But he wouldn't endanger our lives by makin' an attack pellmell...life was dear to him.

From Glendolin Damon Wagner's *Old Neutriment* Boston, Ruth Hill Publisher, 1934, P. 161. Phonetic spellings as they appear in Old Neutriment are retained.

MARK KELLOGG

Kellogg was a reporter for the Bismarck Tribune. He was assigned to cover the Sioux expedition of 1876 by Clement A. Lounsbury, founder and publisher of the paper. Kellogg sent the following report to the New York Herald from the mouth of the Rosebud River on June 21, 1876. He was killed with General Custer at the Battle of the Little Big Horn four days later.

And now a word for the most peculiar genius in the army, a man of great hearted friendships and bitter enmities, of quick, nervous temperament, undaunted courage, will and determination; a man possessing electrical mental capacity and of iron frame and constitution; a brave, faithful, gallant soldier, who has warm friends and bitter enemies; the hardest rider, the greatest pusher, with the most untiring vigilance, overcoming seeming impossibilities, and with an ambition to succeed in all things he undertakes; a man to do right, as he construes the right, in every case; one respected and beloved by his followers, who would freely follow him into the "jaws of hell". Of Lieutenant Colonel G.A. Custer I am now writing. Do not think I am overdrawing the picture. The pen picture is true to life, and is drawn not only from actual observance, but from an experience that cannot mislead me.

From the New York Herald July 11, 1876

The Battle of the Little Big Horn

A feeling of urgency prevailed throughout the command as the Custer and Reno battalions moved forward toward the Little Big Horn Valley. All in the command felt the Indians would scatter as soon as they were aware of cavalry in the area. First Lt. Edward S. Godfrey, commanding troop K, is recorded as having said that Custer was possessed that morning with the idea that the Indians would not stand for a daylight attack.[1]

As the Custer and Reno columns moved closer to the Little Big Horn River, scout George Herendeen, out ahead, observed heavy dust clouds about five miles ahead in the valley.[2] This was a strong indication that the Indians were breaking camp. A bit later, Herendeen and Lt. Luther Hare, from a vantage point close to the river, said they observed heavy dust rising downstream and Indians racing about. Herendeen and Hare agreed that if Custer did not hurry the Indians would escape.[3] While on the vantage point, Heredeen looked back up Reno Creek and could see Custer close to the river and coming on at a fast trot.[4] With Custer at the head of the column was interpreter Fred Girard, who translated for the General when the Arikara Indians scouts rode in with reports. Girard and Custer must have observed the dust clouds as well, and been discussing the meaning of the dust as they advanced down Reno Creek, for later that day, while attached to Reno's command, Girard told Reno that Custer believed the Indians were running away.[5]

When the Custer and Reno columns were still a few miles east of the Little Big Horn River, a lone standing tepee came into view. The tepee was on Custer's side of the creek so he motioned Reno over to him. The two columns then rode together toward the tepee. When they reached it, the scouts had already cut it open, and in it, found the body of an Indian warrior who had died as the result of wounds received at the Battle of The Rosebud. There was evidence strewn about indicating Indians had recently occupied the area and had left in a hurry. Suddenly, from a small knoll along the right side of the trail, Girard, pointing down Reno Creek, yelled, "Here are your Indians running like devils."[6] (Girard had spotted a group of about sixty mounted Indians running toward the Little Big Horn River). Expecting Custer to give immediate chase, Girard spurred his animal off the knoll and galloped quickly back to Custer's side.

Custer, in the mean time, had ordered the Indian scouts in pursuit of the Indians Girard had seen. The scouts refused to go. After berating them, Custer turned to his adjutant and instructed him to order Major Reno in pursuit. The Adjutant was to tell Reno that the village was two and a half miles ahead and running, that Reno should attempt to overtake and bring the Indians to battle, and that he could expect support from the whole outfit.[7] Custer ordered Reno to take the scouts with him.[8] Custer kept only Mitch Bouyer and the six Crow scouts with his column. Girard said he felt his duty was with the scouts so he immediately left Custer and posted himself at Reno's side.[9]

As Reno pulled away, Custer ordered two of the Crows, White Swan and Half Yellow Face, to ride to the edge of the bluffs to look around, but, instead of doing so they joined Reno's Battalion. The Crow Scout Curley said White Swan and Half Yellow Face were afraid and did not want to do as Custer had ordered[10] Realizing what had happened, Bouyer took Curley and the three other Crows, White Man Runs Him, Hairy Moccasin and Goes Ahead and went to the edge of the bluffs.

Just after Reno had left, Custer's Chief of Scouts Lt. Charles Varnum came down from a vantage point in the hills to the south of the trail to report to Custer. Before making his report, Varnum asked Custer where Reno was going and Custer replied, to begin the attack. Varnum said that when he made his final report he said to Custer that he guessed he (Custer) could see about all that he (Varnum) could of the situation. Custer said to Varnum: "I don't know, what can you see?" Varnum responded: "The whole valley is full of Indians and you can see them when you take that rise."[11] As he spoke, Varnum pointed to the bluffs to Custer's right front. After making his report, Varnum rode off to join Reno's column and continue his scouting duties.

Custer had ordered his Regimental Adjutant, Lt. Cooke, and one of his most experienced company commanders, Captain Myles Walter Keogh to accompany Reno, monitor his progress and report back to him as the situation clarified. Although there has been speculation that Cooke and Keogh may have gone off with Reno on their own, it is illogical to assume that they would have done so.

Both officer's duties with the Custer command were too important for them to leave. Cooke was the regimental adjutant, he was obliged to remain at his commanding officer's side. Keogh was commanding one of the two battalions Custer had divided his immediate command into that morning. Like Cooke, his responsibilities were too great for him to leave the Custer column of his own volition.

The sending of these two officers with Reno's Battalion, along with the fact that Custer was now advancing without the bulk of the scouts, supports the likelihood that, at this point, it was Custer's intention to follow after Major Reno and wait for the situation to develop before deciding his next move. Although Cooke is said to have told a surprised Reno, "I am going in with the advance and Myles Keogh is coming too,"[12] his remark must have been made in jest for clearly he and Keogh eventually did return and stay with Custer, as their bodies were found with his at the last stand.

Cooke and Keogh advanced with Reno toward the Little Big Horn River. As soon as it was certain that Reno had found a suitable ford, Keogh wheeled his clayback war horse Comanche about and loped back to Custer with a report that Reno was crossing to the west bank of the Little Big Horn. Cooke decided to wait at the ford for Custer, whom he assumed was coming on. In an interview with Custer Battle master-researcher Walter Mason Camp, Private James Wilber, who had crossed the Little Big Horn with the Reno battalion, would later say that during the crossing, Lt. Cooke was sitting on his horse on the river bank. He would add that he did not see Keogh at the crossing.[13]

Reno, now on the west bank of the Little Big Horn, re-formed his battalion in a glade at the river's edge and then led it out to the open plain. Before doing so, Indian scouts came in and reported the hostiles were no longer running; they were now rallying to meet Reno's command. Girard, now riding at Reno's side, said to Reno that Custer must be made aware of this change in Indian behavior for he (Custer) is laboring under the impression the Indians are running away.[14] Reno did not answer Girard.[15] (There was no love lost between the two. While Custer was in Washington, in the spring of 1876, Reno accused Girard of stealing from the Government and fired him from his interpreter's position at Fort Lincoln. When Custer returned from Washington he reinstated Girard. Girard's reinstatement must have severely embarrassed Major Reno and angered him beyond words.)

Assuming Custer was following close behind Reno, Girard, without orders, doubled back in an attempt to reach the General. Girard knew that Custer had to be made aware of this sudden Indian aggressiveness as quickly as possible. When asked at the Reno Court of Inquiry why he wanted Custer to have this information, Girard replied that he thought Custer might want to change his plans—perhaps recall Reno or call in other parties.[16]

There is a knoll on the east bank of the Little Big Horn at the ford Reno used to cross to the west bank. The trail Reno had followed led around that knoll and then dropped abruptly down the bank to the river. Girard, backtracking to find Custer, reached the knoll and started around it. As he rounded the knoll, he met Lt. Cooke coming toward him.[17] Cooke after seeing Reno's command safely cross the Little Big Horn, must have gone back around to the east side of the knoll to there wait for Custer. From that location, Custer could see him and be more easily guided to the ford. While waiting, Cooke must have heard Girard coming back and so started back around the knoll to see who was returning from Reno's ranks.

When they met, Cooke asked Girard what was the matter. Girard replied that he was looking for the General to tell him that the Indians were no longer running, but were coming out in force to meet Reno. Cooke told Girard to return to Reno and he would report to the General.[18] If Cooke had had any idea of waiting at the crossing site for Custer, he quickly abandoned it. Cooke had also ridden at the head of the column and, like Girard, knew that Custer was coming on convinced that the Indians were running away. He knew it was absolutely essential that Custer be made aware of this sudden change in Indian behavior as soon as possible. Cooke quickly spun his big white gelding about and put him in a flat out run back toward the dust that was the Custer column making its way westward toward the Little Big Horn River.

Reno Creek's main channel runs east to west as it flows toward the Little Big Horn River. Approximately one mile from the Little Big Horn it turns north and flows in that direction for a short distance before it again turns to the west and continues its journey toward the Little Big Horn. Reno, having been called over to the north bank of Reno Creek by Custer, above the site of the Lone Tepee, had eventually to cross back over to the south bank of Reno

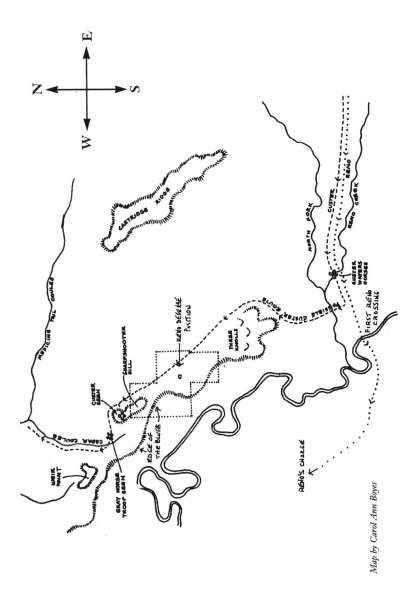

Map by Carol Ann Boyes

Creek, in order to get to his fording place on the Little Big Horn. The most reasonable place for Reno to have made that crossing was somewhere on the main channel of Reno Creek, where it takes its short northerly direction. Custer, following Reno's trail, would naturally come to that same crossing. At the Reno Court of Inquiry, Custer's orderly John Martin testified that Custer's five companies watered their horses somewhere on Reno Creek. The main channel of Reno Creek, then, becomes the logical place for Custer to have stopped to water his horses.

Most researchers believe the watering took place in the North Fork of Reno Creek after Custer had turned away from Major Reno's trail. If we believe orderly John Martin's testimony, that could not be the case. North Fork of Reno Creek basically runs east to west before it joins the main channel. Martin testified that after leaving the watering site, Custer went straight ahead for three hundred yards then turned a bit to the right and went about four or five hundred yards, then turned the bends of some hills and rode up on the bluffs.[19] Martin's description of Custer's movements after leaving the watering site make perfect sense, if Custer watered in the main channel of Reno Creek. If he watered in North Fork, they do not. If the watering had taken place in North Fork, and Custer proceeded as Martin said he did, then the column, after watering, would have been heading east, away from the Little Big Horn and the bluffs. There is further evidence to argue against Custer watering his horses in North Fork. Reno Creek rancher and life-long Custer Battle historian Henry Weibert informed this writer many years ago that by the end of June, the time of the Custer Battle, the North Fork of Reno Creek usually runs dry.

Orderly Martin also gives important testimony about the length of time Custer spent at the watering site. The column, he said, stopped for ten minutes, though the horses were watered in five.[20] Did Custer wait the extra five minutes to give his horses a few minutes rest, or was the delay designed to give Captain Benteen a little more time to close with the main column? We know that Custer knew the approximate location of the Benteen column from the testimony of Chief of Scouts Lt. Charles Varnum who said that on the day of the battle, while scouting ahead, he could not always see the Custer column, but was always aware of its location from the dust it raised.[21]

There can be little doubt that while at the watering site, Custer was still under the impression that the Indians were running away, for while there he sent his compliments to the officers with instructions not to let the horses drink too much as there was much hard riding ahead that day.[22] Custer's instructions indicate clearly that he felt the 7th Cavalry might be in for a "chase" before the day was through.

When Custer left the watering site he continued following Major Reno's trail toward the ford at the Little Big Horn. Suddenly, Lt. Cooke, easily recognized by his white horse and long dundreary beard, appeared coming toward the column in a big hurry. Custer knew something important had happened up ahead. He slowed the column to a walk and finally to a halt as Cooke reined up in front of him. Cooke told Custer that Girard had come back and reported the Indians were now coming out in force to meet Reno's Command. Good or bad, this was the type of news Custer had been waiting for. He now had something tangible to go by.

Custer sat still for a moment on his beautiful stocking legged mare Vic, thinking things through. By all accounts Custer was an exceptionally quick thinker. He once wrote a friend, "First be sure you're right, then go ahead! I ask myself, is it right? Satisfied that it is so, I let nothing swerve me".[23] Custer would act no differently this day on the Little Big Horn.

In his lightening thoughts, Custer must have reflected on the fact that Indians did not usually defend a village when attacked by cavalry—villages were easily replaced and not worth fighting and dying for. He must have asked himself what could account for this change in usual Indian behavior. Tremendous amounts of dust were seen rising from the village, and Girard had actually seen Indians running away. To a veteran Indian campaigner, the logical conclusion would have been that the village and its inhabitants were indeed in flight, and that the warriors coming out to meet Reno were doing so to buy time for the fleeing villagers.

Custer had now made up his mind. Reno was about to engage a rear guard. Custer was not going to accommodate the Indians by getting involved in any such delaying action while the village was escaping. He would let Reno engage the rear guard and he would lead his column down stream after the fleeing village. Once he cut off the village's retreat, the pressure would be off Reno. Warriors engaging Reno would have to leave him and come to the aid of the village's inhabitants. If he could get to the north quickly, he might catch the warriors between the two columns. Believing this to be the case, Custer left Reno's trail and made a bee line to the north.

There is speculation that Custer may have turned away from Reno because of mounted Indians seen on the bluffs to the north by Sgt. Daniel Knipe, of Tom Custer's C Company. Knipe reported the sighting to his First Sergeant, who immediately informed his Company Commander Tom Custer, who in turn relayed the information on to the General. In a Walter Camp interview, Lt. Winfield Scott Edgerly, an officer with the Benteen column, said that several of Reno's officers had told him that the Indians seen on the bluffs were the reason Custer abandoned Reno's trail. This information, volunteered by Edgerly, can not be relied upon since none of Reno's officers were with the Custer column.

It seems highly unlikely, anyway, that Custer would be lending support to Major Reno by going after a group of mounted Indians outside the village. It was cavalry procedure, at that time, when attacking an Indian village, to attempt to drive Indians out of their villages' with the opening charge. After the warriors were out, the village and its contents could be destroyed, forcing the Villagers to return to their reservations. Custer had helped to establish this tactic when he attacked Black Kettle's Cheyenne Village on the Washita River in 1868. Warriors who had survived the initial charge left that Washita Village and from the surrounding hills watched Custer raze the village and it's contents. The Indians seen on the bluffs at the Little Big Horn were already out of the village, why would Custer want to force them back in? It would have been completely contrary to his Washita experience.

That Custer was in a big hurry as he headed north was later confirmed by two troopers who had been sent to the rear with messages, Sgt. Daniel Knipe and Pvt. John Martin. It was further confirmed by the few troopers who were forced out of Custer's advance because their horses had played out.

Hustling north, Custer led his five companies at an angle quartering toward the bluffs. He passed just a bit east of the defensive position Reno would eventually establish on the bluffs. He soon reached a point just below and on the east side of the ridge line now identified as Sharpshooter Ridge. Sharpshooter Ridge lies about a quarter mile back from the edge of the bluffs that overlook the Little Big Horn.

There has been debate about whether Custer, going north, traveled along the edge of the bluffs or the back-side of them. The evidence points to the back-side of Sharpshooter Ridge as the route Custer used to go north. No one ever claimed they saw Custer's trail along the edge of the bluffs and General Terry, in his official report, expressly placed Custer's trail on the back-side of them. The Crow scout Curley adds to the evidence by telling us that while the scouts rode north on the edge of the bluffs, Custer's column rode a bit behind and to the east of the scouts.[24] There is other testimony that you will soon read that adds to the evidence that Custer did ride north on the back-side of Sharpshooter Ridge.

Since Bouyer and the Crows had left the column and gone ahead to the edge of the bluffs, Custer was riding north blind, so to speak. Therefore, when the column reached the northern end of Sharpshooter Ridge, Custer found it necessary to halt the advance momentarly and go to some high point where he could see the lay of the land ahead. He needed to locate an avenue that would take him most directly to the valley floor. In one motion, he raised his right arm to halt the column and put spurs to Vic as he neck-reined her toward the ridge line above. Racing with him to the crest of the ridge was his orderly John Martin, his brother Tom and his nephew Autie Reed. Arriving there, Custer saw that Bouyer and the Crow Scouts had kept pace with him. They were over on the edge of the bluffs opposite the column. When Bouyer spotted Custer on Sharpshooter Ridge, he waved his hat in a rallying salute. Custer returned Bouyer's enthusiastic gesture by doffing his own broad-brimmed hat and waving it in the air.

Custer, however, saw much more from the top of Sharpshooter than Bouyer and his Crow's...he saw the village for the first time. It was enormous. The size of it surely startled him. The fact that it was still standing, however, more than compensated for the shock of its size. Custer was elated. His rapid movement had paid off. The village had not had time to run. He had caught it by surprise. Reno had not yet reached the village. Custer reasoned he was still dealing with the Indians who had come out to meet him.

Considering the size of the village and the fact that it was still standing, Custer would now have realized that sending Reno may have been a mistake. It had, however, turned into a stoke of luck. Reno's appearance to the south had apparently pulled the warriors out of the village leaving it without fighting men. The village, as it now stood, appeared to be vulnerable. Custer's luck seemed to be holding. If he could get down to the valley floor in a hurry he could, perhaps, get into the village without a serious fight.

The warriors who were then engaging Reno would be caught between the two commands. Custer turned to his men, who were halted just below the crest of the ridge, and hollered down, "We've got 'em boys".[25]

In later testimony, orderly John Martin stated that Custer, when he first viewed the village, remarked, "The Indians are asleep in their tepees." Martin, an Italian immigrant, not familiar with American colloquialisms misinterpreted the remark. What Custer perhaps said was, "We've caught them napping".[26] This misinterpretion of Custer's remark has for years helped to confuse the issue. With the information Custer previously had about the warriors sudden aggressiveness, it would be absurd to think that Custer believed the warriors were now asleep in their tents. Indian accounts consistently agree that with Reno's sudden appearance to the south of the camp, the camp's inhabitants were in a turmoil preparing to meet his attack.[27]

What follows here is important in helping to establish Custer's route to the valley floor. Many researchers, have placed Custer on the edge of the bluffs when he first viewed the Indian village. Caretakers of the Little Big Horn National Monument, The National Park Service, even have a marker on the edge of the bluffs where Custer was supposedly last seen. But those who place Custer on the edge of the bluffs, do so as a result of testimony from several of Reno's men, who claimed they saw Custer there while they were fighting in the valley. Reno's eye witnesses may have seen Custer, but if they thought they saw him on the edge of the bluffs they were mistaken.

Looking toward the bluffs, from Reno's position in the valley, anything standing on Sharpshooter Ridge

Weir Point

Valley of the Little Big Horn
Site of the great indian village

Trees that line the river

The upper reaches of Cedar Coulee

Edge of the bluffs of The Little Big Horn

From Reno's position in the valley this little tree on Sharpshooter Ridge appears to be on the edge of the bluffs

CUSTER'S VIEW OF THE LITTLE BIG HORN VALLEY FROM SHARPSHOOTER RIDGE
Author's Photo9

appears to be on the edge of the bluffs. The way the ridges line up creates an optical illusion.[28] Martin, who was on the vantage point with Custer, said that from where they got their first view of the village, they could see the trees and the tepees but could not see the river.[29] That is the view from Sharpshooter Ridge today, as it was in 1876. Martin added that they could not see the entire north end of the village because a high ridge (Weir point) to the northwest blocked their view. Again, this is the view from Sharpshooter Ridge. (see map on page 89)

While on Sharpshooter, Custer could not help but notice the steep draw a bit to the northwest. The draw led down to lower ground. Custer signaled his column up and over the northern edge of Sharpshooter Ridge. The movement placed the column squarely at the upper reaches of the draw he had seen from the vantage point. Martin testified that the entire column was not on the vantage point with Custer, but did pass over it.[30] When Reno's men in the valley observed the gray horses of E troop moving along the bluffs,[31] they were really seeing Custer's column crossing Sharpshooter. The grays stood out, while the bays and sorrels blended in against the countryside.

The draw that Custer saw on the west side of Sharpshooter, is today identified as Cedar Coulee. The coulee was so named because of the perfusion of cedar trees in it. Cedar Coulee is a narrow defile leading down to a wide dry ravine called Medicine Tail Coulee. Medicine Tail is a major drainage that leads to a natural ford on the Little Big Horn River. After the column crossed Sharpshooter Ridge, Custer led it down Cedar Coulee toward Medicine Tail Coulee. At the western terminus of

Medicine Tail was the ford that Custer was seeking to access the village.

Anticipating action soon, Custer wanted the reserve ammunition brought to the front as quickly as possible. Shortly before sighting the village, Custer had sent Sgt. Daniel Knipe to the rear with a message to the packtrain commander to bring the packs to him straight across country. He added that if any of the packs became loose they were to be cut away and abandoned.[32] Custer wanted no delay. As the column made its way down Cedar Coulee, Custer, in his continuing anxiety, shouted over his shoulder for his orderly to go to the rear, find Captain Benteen, tell him it is a big village, to come quick, and bring the ammunition packs.[33]

Upon receipt of the spoken order, Martin shouted, "Yes, Sir" and checked his horse. As he started to turn to the rear, Custer's adjutant, Lt. Cooke, pulling out his notebook, called to Martin: "Wait orderly, I'll give you the message."[34] In the excitement of the moment, the cool headed Cooke recognized that Martin might have trouble repeating the message as stated, so he hastily wrote the now famous last message to Captain Benteen:

Benteen—
Come on, Big Village, Be quick, Bring Packs.

W. W. Cooke
P. S. Bring Pacs (sic)

CAPTAIN
FREDERICK
BENTEEN
West Point Archives

Tearing the page from his notebook, Cooke handed the message to Martin with the additional instruction to return to the command after delivering the note if it was safe to do so; if it was not safe, he was to stay with Benteen and return to his post when the two commands came together.[35] Martin pushed the note into his blouse pocket, leaned forward in the saddle and kicked his tired animal's flanks several times to get him moving.

Martin's remembrance of Custer's "spoken" order included the word "ammunition" before the word "packs".[36] The word, ammunition was not encluded in Cooke's written message. Perhaps in the urgency of the moment, Cooke did not hear the meaning-filled word or simply in haste did not include it in the written order. There can be little doubt that if the written message had asked for the ammunition packs, Benteen would have completly understood the situation and would have responded as Custer must have expected he would.

With Martin's departure we have our last piece of soldier eyewitness information concerning the movements of Custer's five companies, as no soldier in Custer's immediate command would return to tell the story. From that moment, the route that brought Custer to his last stand on the heights overlooking the Little Big Horn Valley, becomes only speculation. Many years have been spent by many people using Indian testimony, artifacts and their own logic to trace Custer's movements. No theories have been proven, though many have possibilities.

Of the countless Indian witnesses of Custer's last battle, there are special problems making their reports, at the last, hopelessly incongruous. An Indian fought as an individual, such that he could attest only to what he saw in the area where he was fighting. Compounding this was the difference between the white man's and Indian's concept of space and time. Indians usually identified a location by the features of the terrain or by some event that had happened there. They referred to time by the position of the sun or the phases of the moon. To account for large numbers of people, they might pick up a handful of grass and scatter it along the ground. In his later years, General Hugh Scott, a July, 1876 replacement for the 7th Cavalry's decimated officers' corp and a veteran of many years service on the frontier with the 7th Cavalry, was asked to reconcile the available Indian accounts of the battle of the Little Big Horn. General Scott, an expert on the Indian sign and spoken language, made an attempt to do so, but finally gave up with the comment that the Indian accounts were irreconcilable.[37]

When perception and language were not a problem, mistrust could be. An Indian could tell a proficient interpreter what he'd seen or done and the information could be quite accurately passed on to a white interviewer— or an interpreter could be told what the Indian determined the interviewer wanted to hear or what the Indian wanted him to hear. The Indian figured it was safer that way. Many Indians were afraid of reprisals for the death of Long Hair Custer. And as late as the fiftieth anniversary of the battle, held at Custer Battlefield on June 25th, 1926, a good number refused to take part because of their continuing fear of punishment.

Thus, we return to Martin, and events that have not been given enough serious consideration by Custer Battle buffs and historians—events that can never provide the missing pieces to the Little Big Horn puzzle, but which are important in helping to establish Custer's mindset. And when we return to Martin, we do so mindful that as a recent Italian immigrant with less than full mastery of the English language, the reliability of his reports might be questioned. Still, Giovanni Martini, who emigrated from his native Italy in 1873 and joined the army in 1874, was more likely to have had trouble constructing a lie than telling the truth. Make mistakes? Yes, he might. But prevaricate? No. Moreover, what possible motive could Martin have had for not telling the truth? It is also difficult to imagine that Martin would have been assigned as orderly to the commanding officer if he was not a soldier of reliable character.[38]

What, then, do we learn from John Martin? We learn that Custer was in some sort of fire fight as soon as he reached Medicine Tail Coulee. We are also told by Martin that when he was sent back to find Captain Benteen, he was told to go over the same trail the column had passed over, therefore he eventually came to the same ridge where he and Custer had first viewed the Indian village. While on the ridge, he paused for a moment to look down at the valley below and saw Reno's troopers fighting the Indians.

When Martin reached the Benteen column, Benteen asked him where Custer was. Martin replied that he supposed by that time he [Custer] had made a charge through the village.[39] Benteen would later claim that Martin told him the Indians were, skedaddling.[40] Whatever the conversation between the two, it seems to have lessened the urgency of Custer's written order in Benteen's mind and lulled Benteen into a state of complacency. In a letter written to his wife just after the battle, Benteen said that as he neared the Little Big Horn River he went ahead to look things over himself because "so much of the Italian trumpeter's story, hadn't panned out."[41] Incrediably, it appears, Benteen had placed more credence in Martin's oral response to his questions then he had in the written order Martin had just delivered to him.[42] If ever there was proper reason for a court martial, it was demonstrated here.

Martin testified that while on Sharpshooter Ridge, he met Boston Custer who was riding alone and on his way forward to join his brother. When they met, Boston asked Martin where the general was? Martin, turned in his saddle, pointed down Cedar Coulee, and said he could find him around the bend at the foot of the draw.[43] Boston immediately spurred on past Martin and disappeared into Cedar Coulee. Before meeting Martin, Boston had passed Benteen who was back on the command's trail and coming on. Members of Benteen's battalion reported they exchanged waves with Boston as he passed some distance off to the right of the trail. Knowing Boston reached his brother we can be certain that General Custer was made aware by Boston that Benteen was within supporting distance and coming on. We can, furthermore, conclude that Custer had reason, now, to assume that his urgent message would get through to Benteen.

Of further significance in the Boston, Martin meeting, is the fact that Boston probably saw the same things Martin saw in the valley vis-a-vis Major Reno. It is not unreasonable then to conclude that Custer, while in the upper reaches of Medicine Tail Coulee, believed Reno was fighting in the valley still expecting to be supported.

What exactly did happen to the Custer column as it entered Medicine Tail Coulee? The most plausible scenario to explain the firing heard by Martin seems to rest on the possible presence there of the mounted Indians Sgt. Knipe had earlier seen on the bluffs. Knipe's Indians had disappeared by the time the Custer column reached the area where they had been seen. They did not go south, or the Crows scouts who were moving north along the edge of the bluffs would have seen them. The only answer seems to be that they went north intending to use the ford at the foot of Medicine Tail to get back to the village. When Custer turned the bend at the foot of Cedar Coulee into Medicine Tail, he probably ran into them and an exchange of gun fire took place. We know that Indians were in the area because John Martin said that he had seen Indians just after leaving the Custer column. He added that they had fired at him. When he did finally reach Benteen Martin was informed that his horse had been wounded in the hip and was bleeding profusely. After briefly engaging Custer in Medicine Tail, the Indians probably broke off and went down toward the ford.

Custer hesitated a bit in the upper reaches of Medicine Tail Coulee, certain that Benteen's arrival was only minutes away. With the addition of Benteen's three companies and the pack train's escort, Custer's battalion strength would improve to over four hundred and fifty men making it a formidable attacking force. Custer would also have the twenty four thousand rounds of reserve ammunition carried by the pack train. After a brief wait, Custer started down Medicine Tail expecting Benteen to come up behind him at any moment.

After Custer left Sharpshooter Ridge, Bouyer and Curley remained on the edge of the bluffs, the other Crows, White Man Runs Him, Goes Ahead and Hairy Moccasin left Bouyer and Curley and rode south. Bouyer and Curly then rode further north to the high ridge now identified as Weir Point.[44] From there they could continue to monitor the village and would be able to see Custer as he came down Medicine Tail Coulee. While sitting on the higher elevation, Curley said that he and Bouyer watched Reno fighting in the valley.[45]

Reno had started his charge on the Indian village with two companies on line and one following in reserve. As the ground began to melt away under the horse's thundering hoofs, the valley suddenly became alive with mounted warriors. It became clear to Reno that he was in for a fight, so he ordered the reserve company up on line and continued the charge[46] About a half mile from the village, Reno signaled a halt. He felt the Indians in his front were becoming too numerous for his small command to handle. He ordered his men to dismount, form a skirmish line across the valley floor and advance on foot. It was reported the move was smartly done. The skirmish line was anchored to a stand of timber at the river's edge. Every fourth man, in each set of fours, was ordered to take his mount, and three others, to the protection of the trees that anchored the right of the line. After a short forward movement, the Indians began to turn the left flank of the line, and so the troopers halted their advance and began to fall back to the trees where the battalion's horses were being held.

Reno, now ensconced in the timber and displaying a certain amount of nervous timidity, became altogether rattled when Custer's favorite Indian scout Bloody Knife was killed at his side. A well placed Indian bullet had penetrated Bloody Knife's skull, splattering blood and brains over Reno's face and tunic. That traumatic occurrence, plus the fact that Custer was nowhere in sight, caused Reno to panic. He ordered his men to mount and then led them on an undisciplined retreat to the bluffs on the east side of the Little Big Horn River. The uncovered retreat resulted in heavy loss of life. Reno's hurried exit from the field also left a good number of troopers behind in the timber. From their perch on the high ground, Curley claimed that he and Bouyer not only saw Reno fighting in the valley but also saw his disastrous retreat to the bluffs on the east side of the Little Big Horn.[47]

Custer was now advancing down Medicine Tail toward the village. When Bouyer saw Custer coming, he raced down from the bluffs to meet him. Curley stayed right along side the older scout. Bouyer knew that Custer, unaware of Reno's retreat, could be heading toward the same type disaster that befell Reno. (Earlier that morning, while on the Divide, Bouyer had warned Custer that there were too many Indians ahead. Bouyer had said that if he was wrong about that Custer could hang him. Custer had responded: "a damned lot of good that would do.")[48] Curley said that when Bouyer arrived at Custer's side the two had a long talk.[49] Curley, could not speak or understand English, therefore Bouyer must have told Curley the essence of the conversation. Curley later reported that Custer had told Bouyer that he was waiting for the other soldiers, and Bouyer had replied that he did not think they would come; that they had been scared out.[50] Bouyer's response to Custer gives credence to Curley's statement that he and Bouyer did see Reno's panicky retreat from the valley.

When Custer learned of Reno's defeat, it must have shaken him badly. The whole operation was now in serious trouble. Going on to attack the village was out of the question. Custer surely guessed why Benteen had failed to come on as ordered. He would have reasoned that Benteen had become aware of Reno's disastrous retreat and had stopped to help Reno restore order in his command. Of course, that is exactly what did happen. It would take some time now, Custer must have thought, but for certain Benteen and the pack train, along with Reno's blooded battalion, would be soon heading north to join him.

Custer needed to put the regiment back together. The low ground in Medicine Tail Coulee was no place to do that. Custer decided to leave Medicine Tail and go to the higher ground to the north. He would there wait for his scattered command to join him. They never came.

Shortly after Benteen arrived on the bluffs, and bolstered Reno's demoralized command, there was the sound of heavy gun fire coming from down-stream. Most enlisted men and officers in Reno's command said they had heard the guns and believed it was Custer in action. Suddenly, two volleys, faint, but distinct, were heard. Captain Godfrey, who even had a hearing deficiency, testified that he heard the volleys fired.[51] Strangely, Captain Benteen and Major Reno swore they had not heard the volleys when questioned about them at the Reno Court of Inquiry.[52] Curley, who, at this point, was still with the Custer column, made reference to volley firing in a Walter Camp interview. He said that at some point during the Custer fight, all in the command were ordered to load and fire together and it occurred to him that it must be a signal. He went on to say there seemed to be some understanding or system about it.[53] The volley firing must have been a signal from Custer to let Benteen know exactly where the command was.

Custer had good reason to now believe Benteen and Reno, together, would be heading towards him. Certainly they should have been able to identify his location by the heavy sound of the soldiers 45/70 carbines, which was quite distinctive from the Indians lighter weapons. Considering all possibilities, the volley firing may well have been simply a signal of distress. Whatever it was, it fell on deaf ears. Benteen and Reno would wait for the pack train to come up before attempting to move in the direction Custer was thought to have gone. While his two subordinates waited, Custer and his entire command perished on a lonely hillside four miles to their north.

Sometime, while Custer was fighting north of Medicine Tail Coulee, the Crow scout Curley slipped away from the command and saved himself. There have been many versions of Curley's miraculous escape from the battlefield, the most popular of which was that he had wrapped himself in a Sioux blanket and skulked away. When Walter Camp asked Curley how he had cheated death, Curley said that when the situation became truly desperate, both Bouyer and Tom Custer told him that he should try and save himself.[54] Curley, said to Bouyer that he would try if he [Bouyer] would go with him. Bouyer said that he was too badly wounded and would stay with the soldiers and fight it out, even though he thought they would all be killed.[55] Curley, then, simply got on a horse and rode away through the hostile Indian ranks unnoticed.

Sometime after the pack train arrived on the bluffs, Benteen and Reno made an effort to go to Custer, but it was too late. After advancing downstream perhaps two miles, Indians, returning to renew the fight with Reno after Custer and his entire command had been killed, forced Reno and his men back to their first defensive position on the bluffs. There they would stay and defend themselves until rescued by General Terry when he arrived on the scene two days later.

There have been countless scenarios offered by knowledgeable and dedicated historians suggesting how General Custer fought his last battle. In truth, however, we shall never know exactly how he and every man in his five companies perished at the Little Big Horn.

If it is my lot to fall in the service of my country...I will have no regrets

—GEORGE ARMSTRONG CUSTER
Cavalryman
1839 - 1876

CHAPTER FIVE
Epilogue

COLONEL J. H. KIDD

6th Michigan Cavalry

> His tragic death at the Little Big Horn
> crowned his career with a tragic interest that
> will not wane while history or tradition
> endure. Hundreds of brave men shed tears
> when they heard of it - men who served under
> and learned to love him in the trying times of
> the Civil War.

From Kidd's address at the unveiling of the Custer
Monument in Monroe, Michigan in 1910.

GENERAL THOMAS L. ROSSER, C.S.A.

*General Rosser was deeply grieved by the death of his friend Custer. In an article
written soon after The Battle of The Little Big Horn he stated:*

> I should like to be commissioned to avenge the
> death of my gallant friend and old enemy, but
> to do so I should like to go back to old Virginia
> and get my division, who once fought him, and
> who like myself, have learned to resect, honor,
> and appreciate the high soldierly qualities and
> exalted manhood of General Custer.

The above appeared in the Army and Navy Journal, July 22,
1876.

PRIVATE JOHN MARTIN

Unites States 7th Cavalry

Martin served as General Custer's Orderly/Trumpeter on the day Custer was killed. He carried Custer's famous last message to Captain Benteen. He was the last soldier to see Custer alive and survive.

I admired General Custer very much; all the men did. He was a fighter and not afraid of anything. But he tried to do more then he could that day. They were too many for us, and good fighters, too. They had better weapons than we had and they knew the ground. It is lucky that any of us escaped alive. I don't think we would but for the fact that they heard that General Terry was coming. I am an old man now and have served the United States a long time since I came from Italy in 1873. I enlisted in 1874 and was in the army for thirty years. My memory isn't as good as it used to be, but I can never forget the battle of the Little Big Horn and General Custer.

I have two sons in the army, and one of them is named for the General. I want them to be good soldiers as their father was.

It's a long time since I rode with Custer to his last fight - forty six years - but I still have the old trumpet that I blew officers' call with the morning of that fatal day, and I still have a lively and deep recollection of, as I have a deep affection for, my old General.

The above statements are from the original affidavit of John Martin signed in the presence of Colonel W.A. Graham in Brooklyn, New York, June 12th, 1922. The affidavit may be found in the Lawrence A. Frost Private Collection, Monroe, Michigan.

GENERAL GEORGE B. McCLELLAN

Former Cammanding General, Army of the Potomac

As a man I mourn in your noble husband's death the loss of a warm unselfish and devoted friend, As a soldier and a citizen I lament the death of one of the most brilliant ornaments of the service and the Nation - a most able and gallant soldier, a pure noble gentleman. At my time of life I can ill afford to lose such a soldier and such a citizen.

It is some consolation to me - I cannot doubt it is to you - that he died as he had lived , a gallant gentleman, a true hero, fighting unflinchingly to the last against desperate odds. death was as he would have it, with his face to the foe, encouraging his men to the last.

The first time I saw your husband to know him was when he was reported to me as having accomplished an act of desperate gallantry on the banks of the Chickahominy. I sent for him at once, and, after thanking him, asked what I could do for him. He seemed to attach no importance to what he had done, and desired nothing. Whereupon I asked if he would like to come upon my staff as a captain. He gladly assented, and remained with me until I was relieved of my command.

He has not lived or died in vain, for rest assured that his long record of brilliant service and the manner of his death will long serve as a model for those who have the true instincts of a cavalry soldier. I am sure that when the true history of that last battle is known it will plainly appear the Custer did precisely what he ought.

The above quotes were taken from a letter, written to Elizabeth Custer after General Custer's death at the Little Big Horn. They may be found in Margurite Merrington's, *The Custer Story*, The Devin-Adair Company, New York, N.Y. 1950 p.327.

SGT. WILLIAM O. TAYLOR

D Troop, 7th Cavalry

Custer was not given to lagging or round about ways. He wanted to get into the fight as soon as he could, and his actions after the first clash might be judged, I think, from this viewpoint. He believed Reno to be fighting at the other end of the camp and was driving the Indians and would continue to fight, as he had ordered Benteen to join him (and be quick) he had every reason to expect his appearance at any minute...but Reno proved incompetent and Benteen showed his indifference ...both failed Custer, and he had to fight it out alone.

The above quote may be found in Fraiser and Robert Hunt, *I Fought With Custer*, Charles Scribner & Son, New York, 1947 p.p. 201-202

PRIVATE DAVID E. DAWSEY

D Troop United States 7th Cavalry

> It is not often a soldier wastes tears over an
> officer but I saw many an old hand wipe his
> eyes with his blouse sleeve [we had no hander-
> chiefs] the day we buried Custer.

The above quote may be found in Robert J. Ege *Settling
The Dust*, Chinook, Montana, 1968, First unnumbered
page.

J.T.HASKELL

Company H, 2nd Ohio Volunteer Cavalry

> The name and fame of General George
> Armstrong Custer are to firmly fixed in the his-
> tory of our glorious Country, and in the hearts
> of her citizens to be even tarnished by the
> snarling Curs of jealousy and hate that now are
> barking at his heels. For the name of General
> George Armstrong Custer is one of the
> few...the immortal names that were not born to
> die.

The above was taken from a letter to T.W. Hill from J.T.
Haskell dated June 19, 1915. Both were attorneys. Both
served in Custer's 3rd Division during the Civil War. The
letter may be found in the Elizabeth Custer Collection,
Little Big Horn Battlefield, Crow Agency, Montana.

EDWARD H. WRIGHT

Served with Custer in The Civil War

During the time I served with him [Custer] he was conspicuous for gallantry in battle and skill and coolness in leading scouting parties. He was the beau-ideal of a cavalry officer, always alert, full of spirit, and delighted to be sent on dangerous assignment.

There was a method in his peculiarities of dress which made him a conspicuous and familiar figure to the men, and he was always where men expected to see their officers. If he was rash, as some are pleased to say, it was rashness born of necessity, when delay meant defeat, and action might lead to victory. I always found him modest, but spirited, incapable of professional jealousy, prompt to assist with his knowledge his less favored associates yet at school in the art of war, kindly and generous, never facing the enemy in anger or hatred but with a joyous courage inspired by a love of his profession and a deep sense of duty.

I met him after the war just before he left for the west on his last march. I was impressed by his sadness, and touched by his affectionate remembrance of many of his old comrades. I knew him best when he was in the full glow of manly and patriotic militarism during the first years of the war, and I felt in him the personification of a manhood tried and proved by the fire of four years of marching and battle. I shall always remember him with admiration and love.

The preceding quotes may be found in a letter to Elizabeth Custer from Edward Wright dated April 30, 1888. The letter is in the Elizabeth Custer Collection, Little Big Horn Battlefield, Crow Agency, Montana.

JACOB GREENE

Served as Custer's Adjutantin the Michigan Brigade during The Civil War

> Since the news of your husband's death I am continually going over the scenes of our service together. I well remember how I was perpetually dreading his death, and that it seemed to me that I could never serve with another officer. And as he went into one danger after another and came out unharmed, ...I began to feel that the man bore a charmed life.

> I never loved and admired any other man as I did your husband. What he was to you and you were to him I well know. You were the first and only love of one of the bravest, strongest and noblest of men, whose mark in the history of this Country and his profession will never be lost, and whose death was the seal of a record, the most brilliant in deeds without a stain of dishonor.

The above quotes may be found in Lawrence A. Frost's, *General Custer's Libbie*, Superior Publishing Co., Seattle 1976, p.11.

PRIVATE AMI F. MULFORD

7th United States Cavalry

> Custer was a fighter, a kind commander, and a gentleman in every sense of the word. Custer did not want a detail at the close of a hard days march, to put his tent up and wait for him. No, not he. "Boys, make your selves as comfortable as you can" was all he wanted at that time. He would eat hardtack and bacon and roll in his blanket under the nearest bush or tree, and fall asleep, but it did not take much to wake him up, and when his eyes were open he was awake all over! "Follow me boys" was his order for a charge, and who would not follow such a commander?

The above quote may be found in *Fighting Indians in Custer's 7th Cavalry*, Corning N.Y., n.p., p. 67.

GENERAL NELSON A. MILES

After Custer's defeat at the Little Big Horn, General Miles was sent with his 5th infantry to patrol the Yellowstone in order to prevent the Indians from crossing the river and going north. Miles eventually became convinced that the efforts of that summer were doomed to failure. In August he wrote to his wife:

> The more I see of movements here the more admiration I have for Custer and I am satisfied his likes will not be found very soon again.

GENERAL
NELSON A.
MILES

Brian C. Pohanka
Collection

The above quote may be found in Robert M. Utley and WilcombE. Washburn's *The American Heritage History of the Indian Wars*. American Heritage Publishing Co.,Inc, New York, 1978,p. 301.

MAJOR JOSEPH TILFORD

7th Cavalry

Tilford, a senior major in the 7th Cavalry, was on detached service and was not with the regiment at the Little Big Horn. He was sent to the battlefield in 1877 to retreive the bodies of the fallen officers and to transport their remains back to the States for burials in military cemeteries or family plots.

On yesterday I shipped by U.S. Express via Chicago, the remains of your heroic husband Genl. Custer to West Point, N.Y., care of the commanding officer of that Post. Those were my instructions from Genl. Sheridan. I presume an officer will accompany the remains from Chicago on.

It may be some consolation for you to know that I personally superintented the transfer of the remains from the box in which they came from the battlefield to the casket which conveys them to West Point.

I enclose you a lock of hair taken from the remains which are so precious to you. I also kept a few hairs for myself as having been worn by a man who was my beau ideal of a soldier and gentleman.

From a letter to Elizabeth Custer from Major Joseph Tilford dated July 28, 1877. The letter may be found in the Lawrence A. Frost Collection, Monroe, Michigan.

LAWRENCE BARRETT

Eminent actor of the day and close friend of George Armstrong Custer

His career may thus be briefly given: he was born in obscurity; he rose to eminence; denied social advantages in his youth, his untiring industry supplied them; the obstacles to his advancement became the stepping stones to his fortunes; free to choose for good or evil, he choose rightly; truth was his striking characteristic...his acts found his severest critic in his own breast; he was a good son, a good brother, a good and affectionate husband, a Christian soldier, a steadfast friend. Entering the army as a cadet in early youth, he became a general while still on the threshold of manhood; with ability undenied, with valor proved on many a hard fought field, he acquired the affection of the Nation; and he died in action at the age of thirty seven, died as he would have wished to die, no lingering disease preying upon that iron frame. At the head of his command, the messenger of death awaited him; from the field of battle where he had so often directed the storm, his gallant spirit took its flight. Cut off from aid, abandoned in the midst of incredible odds the noble Custer fell, bequeathing to the Nation his sword; to his comrades an example; to his friends a memory, and to his beloved a hero's name.

The above quote may be found in Cyrus Townsend Brady's *Northwest Fights and Fighters* Doubleday, Page and Co. New York, 1913, p. 261.

YOUNG WEST POINT GRADUATES WHO SERVED WITH THE 7TH CAVALRY
AT THE LITTLE BIG HORN

EDWARD S. GODFREY
CLASS OF 1867
COMMANDED COMPANY K
SURVIVED

West Point Archives

JAMES G. STURGIS
CLASS OF 1875
MISSING AND PRESUMED
KILLED

West Point Archives

JAMES E. PORTER
CLASS OF 1869
MISSING AND PRESUMED
KILLED

West Point Archives

LUTHER R. HARE
CLASS OF 1874
SERVED WITH THE SCOUTS
AT THE LITTLE BIG HORN
SURVIVED

West Point Archives

HENRY M. HARRINGTON
CLASS OF 1872
MISSING AND PRESUMED
KILLED

West Point Archives

BENJAMIN H. HODESON
CLASS OF 1870
SERVED AS MAJOR RENO'S
ADJUTANT
KILLED AT
THE LITTLE BIG HORN

West Point Archives

CHARLES VARNUM
CLASS OF 1872
CHIEF OF SCOUTS AT THE
LITTLE BIG HORN
SURVIVED

West Point Archives

WINFIELD S. EDGERLY
CLASS OF 1870
SURVIVED

West Point Archives

GRAVES OF ELIZABETH AND GEORGE CUSTER
POST CEMETERY WEST POINT

114

Footnotes

PREFACE

1. From a letter to Elizabeth Custer from J.B. Kershaw, Major General, C.S.A. Original letter in the Lawrence A. Frost Collection. Monroe, Michigan.

2. From a letter to T. W. Hill from J.T. Haskell, June 29, 1915. The remark was heard by Haskell in a lecture given by General Gordon entitled "The last days of the Confederacy." The original letter is in the Elizabeth Bacon Custer collection, Little Big Horn National Battlefield, Crow Agency, Montana. Sec. C A-19 C-1763. Hereafter Custer Collection, Montana.

3 Marguerite Merington, *The Custer Story* (New York: Devin-Adair,1950)p.143. Hereafter cited as Merington.

4. From a letter to Elizabeth Custer from E.D. Woodbury, February 9, 1924. Custer Collection, Montana. Sec. C A-19 C-1765X.

5. From a letter to Elizabeth Custer from W. H. Beebe, June 18, 1910. Custer Collection, Montana Sec. C A-19 C-1758X. Private Beebe served in Custer's 3rd Division of Sheridan's Cavalry Corp. He was a member of Company G, 3rd New Jersey Cavalry, 2nd Brigade. He was 19 years old when he served under Custer.

6. J. H. Kidd, from his address at the unveiling of the Custer statue in Monroe, Michigan, 1910.

7. From letters signed by officers of the Michigan Brigade requesting transfer to Custer's 3rd Cavalry Division. Custer Collection, Montana. Sec. C A-19 C-1797.

8. Merington, *The Custer Story*, p. 6.

9. Ibid., p. 6.

10. Col. Charles King, *Campaign With Crook* (Franklyn Square, New York: Harper and Bros.) p. 78.

11. W. A. Graham, *The Custer Myth* (New York: Bonanza, 1953) "The Benteen-Golden Letters" p. 189 - 211.

12. This quote by Lt. Varnum can be found written on the margin of a book in the rare book collection at Little Big Horn Battlefield. The book is unnamed here but is easily located in Little Big Horn Battlefield Archives, Crow Agency, Montana. The notation was dated June 4, 1926, and written by George Murray, then Chaplain of the 7th Cavalry. Chaplain Murry and Colonel Varnum had, according to this book, many discussions about the battle before and during the semi-centennial of the Little Big Horn fight

CHAPTER ONE

The Birth of a Legend

1. Henry Howe, *A Talk With John Giles of Scio*, vol. 1 (Norwalk, Ohio. Laning, 1896) p. 900.

2. Milton Ronsheim, *The Life of General Custer*, Custeriana Monograph # 1. Reprinted from the *Cadiz Republican*, Cadiz, Ohio, 1929.

3. From a letter to Elizabeth Custer from William O. Wirt, August 21, 1912. Custer Collection, Montana.

4. Milton Ronshiem, *The Life of General Custer*, Custeriana Monograph # 1. Reprinted from the *Cadiz Republican*, Cadiz, Ohio, 1929. The statement may be found in that part of Mr. Ronshiem's article, *Reminiscences of Custer's Cousin*. Custer's Cousin Mary Snyder stated further on in the article that her recollection of the general was quite good. The reprint is part of the Custeriana Series, Dr. Lawrence A. Frost Collection, Monroe County Library, Monroe, Michigan.

5. Lawrence A. Frost, *General Custer's Libbie* (Seattle: Superior, 1976) p. 114.

6. Marguerite Merington, *The Custer Story* (New York, Devin-Adair, 1950) p.p. 7-8.

7. Joseph Pearson Farley, *West Point in the Early Sixties* (Troy, N.Y.: Pafraets, 1902) p.p. 21-22. Also see Joseph Ellis and Robert Moore, *School for Soldiers*, New York, Oxford University Press, p. 98.

8. W. Donald Horn, Editor, Forward by Blaine L. Beale, *Skinned-The Delinquency Record of Cadet George Armstrong Custer United States Military Academy Class of June 1861*. Don Horn Publications, Short Hills, N.J. 1980. The booklet contains the entire delinquency record of George Custer as recorded while a Cadet at West Point.

9. A. Noel Blakeman, *Service in Personal Recollections of the War of Rebellion* (New York, Putnams, 1897) p. 194.

10. Ibid., p. 194.

11. From a letter to Elizabeth Custer from General E. Van Arsdale Andress, September 27, 1905. Custer Collection, Montana. Reference A-19, C-1792X.

12. Morris Shaff, *The Sunset of the Confederacy* (Boston: John W. Luce and Company, 1912) p. 114.

CHAPTER TWO

The Civil War Years

1. Merington, p. 10.

2. Ibid., p. 12.

3. Ibid., p. 11.

4. George B. McClellan, *Gen. McClellen's Own Story* (New York: Charles L. Webster, 1887) p. 123.

5. Ibid., p. 365.

6. Merington, p. 58.

7. David F. Riggs, *East of Gettysburg* (Bellevue, Nebraska: The Old Army Press, 1970) p. 15. Hereafter cited as Riggs

8. Merington, p. 55.

9. Michael Phipps, "Come on you Wolverines" (House Military Impressions, 401 Baltimore Street, Gettysburg, PA 1995) p 37.

10. Riggs, p. 55.

11. Lawrence A. Frost, *General Custer's Libbie* (Seattle: Superior, 1976) p. 223. Hereafter cited as Frost's Libbie

12. J. H. Kidd, *Historical Sketch of General Custer*, Address at unveiling of the Custer equestrian statue, Monroe, Michigan, June 4, 1910.

13. Riggs, p. 28.

14. Ibid., p. 50.

15. Ibid., p. 50.

16. W. Donald Horn, *Witness for the Defense of General George Armstrong Custer* (Don Horn Publications, Short Hills, N.J. 1981.) p. 96,97,98.

17. Merington, p. 159.

CHAPTER THREE

The Years On The Plains

1. From a letter to Edwin M. Stanton from General Philip H. Sheridan, April 6, 1866. The Custer Collection, Montana, Sec. C A-19 C-1869.

2. Kathrine Gibson Fougera, *With Custer's Cavalry* (Caldwell, Idaho: Caxton, 1940) p. 127.

3. John A. Carroll, *Washita* (Bryan, Texas: Privately Published. 1979) p. 7.

4. Jay Monahgan, *Custer* (Boston, Little, Brown and Co., 1954) p. 305.

5. John M. Carroll, Editor, *General Custer and The Battle of The Washita: The Federal View* (Bryan, Texas: Guidon Press, 1978) p. 38.

6. Merington, .p. 223.

7. Elizabeth Bacon Custer in The Outlook, July 27, 1927.

8. Frost, *Libbie*, p. 216.

9. Ibid., p. 216.

CHAPTER FOUR

The Road to The Little Big Horn

1. Custer Collection Montana, Sec. C A-19 C-2696.

2. Lawrence A. Frost, *General Custer's Libbie* (Seattle: Superior, 1976) p. 223.

3. Lieutenant James H. Bradley, *March of the Montana Column A Prelude to the Custer Disaster*, Edgar I. Stewart, Ed. (Norman OK: University of Oklahoma Press, 1961) p. 143.

4. John S. Gray, *Centennial Campaign* (Fort Collins, CO: Old Army, 1976) p.p. 147-148.

5. General William T. Sherman, The Sherman Papers in the Library of Congress, Washington, D.C.

CHAPTER FIVE

The Battle of The Little Big Horn

1. *Myth* p. 138.

2. Ibid., p. 258

3. Ibid., p. 263

4. Ibid., p. 263

5. Col. W. A. Graham. *The Official Record of a Court of Inquiry Convened by the President of the United States to Investigate the Conduct of Major Marcus A. Reno at the Battle of the Little Big Horn.* W. A. Graham, Pacific Palisades, California, 1951. P. 78. Herafter cited as Reno Court.

6. Ibid., p. 75.

7. Ibid., p. 76.

8. Ibid., p. 76.

9. Ibid., p. 76.

10. Kenneth Hammer, Ed., *Walter Camp Notes on the Custer Fight* (Norman, OK: University of Oklahoma Press) p. 166. Hereafter cited as Custer in'76.

11. John H. Carroll, Ed., *I, Varnum* (Glendale,Ca.: The Arthur Clark Co., 1982) P. 89.

12. *Myth*, p. 228.

13. *Custer in '76*, p.148.

14. *Reno Court*, p. 100.

15. Ibid., p. 100.

16. Ibid., p.p. 100, 117.

17. Ibid., p. 101.

18. Ibid., p. 101.

19. Ibid., p. 341.

20. Ibid., p. 341.

21. *Custer in '76*, p. 61

22. *Reno Court*, p. 340.

23. Merington, p. 65.

24. *Custer in '76*, p. 166.

25. *Reno Court*, p. 351.

26. *Myth*, p. 293.

27. *Myth*, Chapter 5, *The Sioux* p. p. 45-100.

28. Henry Weibert, *Sixty-Six Years in Custer's Shadow* (Billings, Montana: Bannack, 1985) p. 43.

29. *Reno Court*, p. 342.

30. *Reno Court*, p. 342.

31. Ibid., p. 134.

32. *Custer in '76*, p. 94

33. *Myth*, p. 299.

34. Ibid., p. 290.

35. Ibid., p. 290.

36. Ibid., p. 290.

37. Ibid., p. 3.

38. Kenneth HAmmer, *Biographies of the 7th Cavalry June 25, 1876* (Old Army Press, Fort Collins, CO, 1972), p. 158.

39 *Reno Court*, p. 343.

40. *Myth*. P. 180.

41. Ibid., p. 181.

42. Ibid., p. 180.

43. Ibid., p. 290.

44. *Custer in '76*, p. 167.

45. Ibid. p. 166

46. *Reno Court*, p. 500.

47. *Custer in '76*, p. 166.

48. Ibid., p. 61

49. Charles Kuhlman, Ph.D. *Legend into History*, (The Stackpole Company, Harrisburg, PA p 170), p. 170.

50. *Custer in '76*, p. 158.

51. *Myth*, p. 142.

52. *Reno Court*, p. 360 (Benteen) p. 526 (Reno).

53. *Custer in '76*, p. 163.

54. Ibid., p. 165.

55. Ibid., p. 159.